HEBREW

V O C A B U L A R Y

I0170827

FOR ENGLISH SPEAKERS

ENGLISH-HEBREW

The most useful words
To expand your lexicon and sharpen
your language skills

3000 words

Hebrew vocabulary for English speakers - 3000 words

By Andrey Taranov

T&P Books vocabularies are intended for helping you learn, memorize and review foreign words. The dictionary is divided into themes, covering all major spheres of everyday activities, business, science, culture, etc.

The process of learning words using T&P Books' theme-based dictionaries gives you the following advantages:

- Correctly grouped source information predetermines success at subsequent stages of word memorization
- Availability of words derived from the same root allowing memorization of word units (rather than separate words)
- Small units of words facilitate the process of establishing associative links needed for consolidation of vocabulary
- Level of language knowledge can be estimated by the number of learned words

Copyright © 2016 T&P Books Publishing

All rights reserved. No part of this book may be reproduced or utilized in any form or by any means, electronic or mechanical, including photocopying, recording or by information storage and retrieval system, without permission in writing from the publishers.

T&P Books Publishing
www.tpbooks.com

ISBN: 978-1-78716-408-6

This book is also available in E-book formats.
Please visit www.tpbooks.com or the major online bookstores.

HEBREW VOCABULARY
for English speakers

T&P Books vocabularies are intended to help you learn, memorize, and review foreign words. The vocabulary contains over 3000 commonly used words arranged thematically.

- Vocabulary contains the most commonly used words
- Recommended as an addition to any language course
- Meets the needs of beginners and advanced learners of foreign languages
- Convenient for daily use, revision sessions, and self-testing activities
- Allows you to assess your vocabulary

Special features of the vocabulary

- Words are organized according to their meaning, not alphabetically
- Words are presented in three columns to facilitate the reviewing and self-testing processes
- Words in groups are divided into small blocks to facilitate the learning process
- The vocabulary offers a convenient and simple transcription of each foreign word

The vocabulary has 101 topics including:

Basic Concepts, Numbers, Colors, Months, Seasons, Units of Measurement, Clothing & Accessories, Food & Nutrition, Restaurant, Family Members, Relatives, Character, Feelings, Emotions, Diseases, City, Town, Sightseeing, Shopping, Money, House, Home, Office, Working in the Office, Import & Export, Marketing, Job Search, Sports, Education, Computer, Internet, Tools, Nature, Countries, Nationalities and more ...

T&P BOOKS' THEME-BASED DICTIONARIES

The Correct System for Memorizing Foreign Words

Acquiring vocabulary is one of the most important elements of learning a foreign language, because words allow us to express our thoughts, ask questions, and provide answers. An inadequate vocabulary can impede communication with a foreigner and make it difficult to understand a book or movie well.

The pace of activity in all spheres of modern life, including the learning of modern languages, has increased. Today, we need to memorize large amounts of information (grammar rules, foreign words, etc.) within a short period. However, this does not need to be difficult. All you need to do is to choose the right training materials, learn a few special techniques, and develop your individual training system.

Having a system is critical to the process of language learning. Many people fail to succeed in this regard; they cannot master a foreign language because they fail to follow a system comprised of selecting materials, organizing lessons, arranging new words to be learned, and so on. The lack of a system causes confusion and eventually, lowers self-confidence.

T&P Books' theme-based dictionaries can be included in the list of elements needed for creating an effective system for learning foreign words. These dictionaries were specially developed for learning purposes and are meant to help students effectively memorize words and expand their vocabulary.

Generally speaking, the process of learning words consists of three main elements:

- Reception (creation or acquisition) of a training material, such as a word list
- Work aimed at memorizing new words
- Work aimed at reviewing the learned words, such as self-testing

All three elements are equally important since they determine the quality of work and the final result. All three processes require certain skills and a well-thought-out approach.

New words are often encountered quite randomly when learning a foreign language and it may be difficult to include them all in a unified list. As a result, these words remain written on scraps of paper, in book margins, textbooks, and so on. In order to systematize such words, we have to create and continually update a "book of new words." A paper notebook, a netbook, or a tablet PC can be used for these purposes.

This "book of new words" will be your personal, unique list of words. However, it will only contain the words that you came across during the learning process. For example, you might have written down the words "Sunday," "Tuesday," and "Friday." However, there are additional words for days of the week, for example, "Saturday," that are missing, and your list of words would be incomplete. Using a theme dictionary, in addition to the "book of new words," is a reasonable solution to this problem.

The theme-based dictionary may serve as the basis for expanding your vocabulary.

It will be your big "book of new words" containing the most frequently used words of a foreign language already included. There are quite a few theme-based dictionaries available, and you should ensure that you make the right choice in order to get the maximum benefit from your purchase.

Therefore, we suggest using theme-based dictionaries from T&P Books Publishing as an aid to learning foreign words. Our books are specially developed for effective use in the sphere of vocabulary systematization, expansion and review.

Theme-based dictionaries are not a magical solution to learning new words. However, they can serve as your main database to aid foreign-language acquisition. Apart from theme dictionaries, you can have copybooks for writing down new words, flash cards, glossaries for various texts, as well as other resources; however, a good theme dictionary will always remain your primary collection of words.

T&P Books' theme-based dictionaries are specialty books that contain the most frequently used words in a language.

The main characteristic of such dictionaries is the division of words into themes. For example, the *City* theme contains the words "street," "crossroads," "square," "fountain," and so on. The *Talking* theme might contain words like "to talk," "to ask," "question," and "answer".

All the words in a theme are divided into smaller units, each comprising 3–5 words. Such an arrangement improves the perception of words and makes the learning process less tiresome. Each unit contains a selection of words with similar meanings or identical roots. This allows you to learn words in small groups and establish other associative links that have a positive effect on memorization.

The words on each page are placed in three columns: a word in your native language, its translation, and its transcription. Such positioning allows for the use of techniques for effective memorization. After closing the translation column, you can flip through and review foreign words, and vice versa. "This is an easy and convenient method of review – one that we recommend you do often."

Our theme-based dictionaries contain transcriptions for all the foreign words. Unfortunately, none of the existing transcriptions are able to convey the exact nuances of foreign pronunciation. That is why we recommend using the transcriptions only as a supplementary learning aid. Correct pronunciation can only be acquired with the help of sound. Therefore our collection includes audio theme-based dictionaries.

The process of learning words using T&P Books' theme-based dictionaries gives you the following advantages:

- You have correctly grouped source information, which predetermines your success at subsequent stages of word memorization
- Availability of words derived from the same root (lazy, lazily, lazybones), allowing you to memorize word units instead of separate words
- Small units of words facilitate the process of establishing associative links needed for consolidation of vocabulary
- You can estimate the number of learned words and hence your level of language knowledge
- The dictionary allows for the creation of an effective and high-quality revision process
- You can revise certain themes several times, modifying the revision methods and techniques
- Audio versions of the dictionaries help you to work out the pronunciation of words and develop your skills of auditory word perception

The T&P Books' theme-based dictionaries are offered in several variants differing in the number of words: 1.500, 3.000, 5.000, 7.000, and 9.000 words. There are also dictionaries containing 15,000 words for some language combinations. Your choice of dictionary will depend on your knowledge level and goals.

We sincerely believe that our dictionaries will become your trusty assistant in learning foreign languages and will allow you to easily acquire the necessary vocabulary.

TABLE OF CONTENTS

PRONUNCIATION GUIDE

Letter's name	Letter	Hebrew example	T&P phonetic alphabet	English example
Alef	א	אריה	[ɑ], [ɑ:]	bath, to pass
	א	אחד	[ɛ], [ɛ:]	habit, bad
	א	מָאָה	[']	glottal stop
Bet	ב	בית	[b]	baby, book
Gimel	ג	גמל	[g]	game, gold
Gimel+geresh	ג׳	ג׳ונגל	[ʤ]	joke, general
Dalet	ד	דג	[d]	day, doctor
Hei	ה	הר	[h]	home, have
Vav	ו	וסת	[v]	very, river
Zayin	ז	זאב	[z]	zebra, please
Zayin+geresh	ז׳	ז׳ורנל	[ʒ]	forge, pleasure
Chet	ח	חוט	[x]	as in Scots 'loch'
Tet	ט	טוב	[t]	tourist, trip
Yud	י	יום	[j]	yes, New York
Kaph	ך כ	בריש	[k]	clock, kiss
Lamed	ל	לחם	[l]	lace, people
Mem	ם מ	מלך	[m]	magic, milk
Nun	ן נ	נר	[n]	name, normal
Samech	ס	סוס	[s]	city, boss
Ayin	ע	עין	[ɑ], [ɑ:]	bath, to pass
	ע	תָשעָים	[']	voiced pharyngeal fricative
Pei	ף פ	פיל	[p]	pencil, private
Tsadi	צ	צעצוע	[ʦ]	cats, tsetse fly
Tsadi+geresh	צ׳	צ׳ק	[ʧ]	church, French
Qoph	ק	קוף	[k]	clock, kiss
Resh	ר	רכבת	[r]	French (guttural) R
Shin	ש	שלחן, עָשׂרָים	[s], [ʃ]	city, machine
Tav	ת	תפוז	[t]	tourist, trip

ABBREVIATIONS
used in the vocabulary

English abbreviations

ab.	-	about
adj	-	adjective
adv	-	adverb
anim.	-	animate
as adj	-	attributive noun used as adjective
e.g.	-	for example
etc.	-	et cetera
fam.	-	familiar
fem.	-	feminine
form.	-	formal
inanim.	-	inanimate
masc.	-	masculine
math	-	mathematics
mil.	-	military
n	-	noun
pl	-	plural
pron.	-	pronoun
sb	-	somebody
sing.	-	singular
sth	-	something
v aux	-	auxiliary verb
vi	-	intransitive verb
vi, vt	-	intransitive, transitive verb
vt	-	transitive verb

Hebrew abbreviations

ז	-	masculine
ז"ר	-	masculine plural
ז, נ	-	masculine, feminine
נ	-	feminine
נ"ר	-	feminine plural

BASIC CONCEPTS

1. Pronouns

I, me	ani	אֲנִי (ז, נ)
you (masc.)	ata	אַתָּה (ז)
you (fem.)	at	אַת (נ)
he	hu	הוּא (ז)
she	hi	הִיא (נ)
we	a'naχnu	אֲנַחְנוּ (ז, נ)
you (masc.)	atem	אַתֶּם (ז״ר)
you (fem.)	aten	אַתֶּן (נ״ר)
you (polite, sing.)	ata, at	אַתָּה (ז), אַת (נ)
you (polite, pl)	atem, aten	אַתֶּם (ז״ר), אַתֶּן (נ״ר)
they (masc.)	hem	הֵם (ז״ר)
they (fem.)	hen	הֵן (נ״ר)

2. Greetings. Salutations

Hello! (fam.)	ʃalom!	שָׁלוֹם!
Hello! (form.)	ʃalom!	שָׁלוֹם!
Good morning!	'boker tov!	בּוֹקֶר טוֹב!
Good afternoon!	tsaha'rayim tovim!	צָהֳרַיִם טוֹבִים!
Good evening!	'erev tov!	עֶרֶב טוֹב!
to say hello	lomar ʃalom	לוֹמַר שָׁלוֹם
Hi! (hello)	hai!	הַיי!
greeting (n)	ahlan	אַהְלָן
to greet (vt)	lomar ʃalom	לוֹמַר שָׁלוֹם
How are you? (form.)	ma ʃlomeχ?, ma ʃlomχa?	מַה שְׁלוֹמֵךְ? (נ), מַה שְׁלוֹמְךָ?(ז)
How are you? (fam.)	ma niʃma?	מַה נִשְׁמָע?
What's new?	ma χadaʃ?	מַה חָדָשׁ?
Bye-Bye! Goodbye!	lehitra'ot!	לְהִתְרָאוֹת!
Bye!	bai!	בַּיי!
See you soon!	lehitra'ot bekarov!	לְהִתְרָאוֹת בְּקָרוֹב!
Farewell!	heye ʃalom!	הֱיֵה שָׁלוֹם!
Farewell! (form.)	lehitra'ot!	לְהִתְרָאוֹת!
to say goodbye	lomar lehitra'ot	לוֹמַר לְהִתְרָאוֹת
So long!	bai!	בַּיי!
Thank you!	toda!	תּוֹדָה!
Thank you very much!	toda raba!	תּוֹדָה רַבָּה!

You're welcome	bevakaʃa	בְּבַקָּשָׁה
Don't mention it!	al lo davar	עַל לֹא דָּבָר
It was nothing	ein be'ad ma	אֵין בְּעַד מָה

| Excuse me! | sliχa! | סְלִיחָה! |
| to excuse (forgive) | lis'loaχ | לִסְלוֹחַ |

to apologize (vi)	lehitnatsel	לְהִתְנַצֵּל
My apologies	ani mitnatsel, ani mitna'tselet	אֲנִי מִתְנַצֵּל (ז), אֲנִי מִתְנַצֶּלֶת (נ)
I'm sorry!	ani mitsta'er, ani mitsta''eret	אֲנִי מִצְטַעֵר (ז), אֲנִי מִצְטַעֶרֶת (נ)
to forgive (vt)	lis'loaχ	לִסְלוֹחַ
It's okay! (that's all right)	lo nora	לֹא נוֹרָא
please (adv)	bevakaʃa	בְּבַקָּשָׁה

Don't forget!	al tiʃkaχ!	אַל תִּשְׁכַּח! (ז)
Certainly!	'betaχ!	בֶּטַח!
Of course not!	'betaχ ʃelo!	בֶּטַח שֶׁלֹּא!
Okay! (I agree)	okei!	אוֹקֵיי!
That's enough!	maspik!	מַסְפִּיק!

3. Questions

Who?	mi?	מִי?
What?	ma?	מָה?
Where? (at, in)	'eifo?	אֵיפֹה?
Where (to)?	le'an?	לְאָן?
From where?	me''eifo?	מֵאֵיפֹה?
When?	matai?	מָתַי?
Why? (What for?)	'lama?	לָמָה?
Why? (~ are you crying?)	ma'du'a?	מַדּוּעַ?

What for?	biʃvil ma?	בִּשְׁבִיל מָה?
How? (in what way)	eiχ, keitsad?	כֵּיצַד? אֵיךְ?
What? (What kind of ...?)	'eize?	אֵיזֶה?
Which?	'eize?	אֵיזֶה?
To whom?	lemi?	לְמִי?
About whom?	al mi?	עַל מִי?
About what?	al ma?	עַל מָה?
With whom?	im mi?	עִם מִי?
How many? How much?	'kama?	כַּמָּה?
Whose?	ʃel mi?	שֶׁל מִי?

4. Prepositions

| with (accompanied by) | im | עִם |
| without | bli, lelo | בְּלִי, לְלֹא |

to (indicating direction)	le...	...לְ
about (talking ~ ...)	al	עַל
before (in time)	lifnei	לִפְנֵי
in front of ...	lifnei	לִפְנֵי

under (beneath, below)	mi'taxat le...	מִתַּחַת לְ...
above (over)	me'al	מֵעַל
on (atop)	al	עַל
from (off, out of)	mi, me	מִ, מְ
of (made from)	mi, me	מִ, מְ

| in (e.g., ~ ten minutes) | tox | תּוֹךְ |
| over (across the top of) | 'derex | דֶּרֶךְ |

5. Function words. Adverbs. Part 1

Where? (at, in)	'eifo?	אֵיפֹה?
here (adv)	po, kan	פֹּה, כָּאן
there (adv)	ʃam	שָׁם

| somewhere (to be) | 'eifo ʃehu | אֵיפֹה שֶׁהוּא |
| nowhere (not anywhere) | beʃum makom | בְּשׁוּם מָקוֹם |

| by (near, beside) | leyad ... | לְיַד ... |
| by the window | leyad haxalon | לְיַד הַחַלּוֹן |

Where (to)?	le'an?	לְאָן?
here (e.g., come ~!)	'hena, lekan	הֵנָה; לְכָאן
there (e.g., to go ~)	leʃam	לְשָׁם
from here (adv)	mikan	מִכָּאן
from there (adv)	miʃam	מִשָּׁם

| close (adv) | karov | קָרוֹב |
| far (adv) | raxok | רָחוֹק |

near (e.g., ~ Paris)	leyad	לְיַד
nearby (adv)	karov	קָרוֹב
not far (adv)	lo raxok	לֹא רָחוֹק

left (adj)	smali	שְׂמָאלִי
on the left	mismol	מִשְּׂמֹאל
to the left	'smola	שְׂמֹאלָה

right (adj)	yemani	יְמָנִי
on the right	miyamin	מִיָּמִין
to the right	ya'mina	יָמִינָה

in front (adv)	mika'dima	מִקָּדִימָה
front (as adj)	kidmi	קָדְמִי
ahead (the kids ran ~)	ka'dima	קָדִימָה

behind (adv)	me'aχor	מֵאָחוֹר
from behind	me'aχor	מֵאָחוֹר
back (towards the rear)	a'χora	אֲחוֹרָה
middle	'emtsa	אָמְצַע (ז)
in the middle	ba''emtsa	בָּאָמְצַע
at the side	mehatsad	מֵהַצַּד
everywhere (adv)	beχol makom	בְּכָל מָקוֹם
around (in all directions)	misaviv	מִסָּבִיב
from inside	mibifnim	מִבִּפְנִים
somewhere (to go)	le'an ʃehu	לְאָן שֶׁהוּא
straight (directly)	yaʃar	יָשָׁר
back (e.g., come ~)	baχazara	בַּחֲזָרָה
from anywhere	me'ei ʃam	מֵאֵי שָׁם
from somewhere	me'ei ʃam	מֵאֵי שָׁם
firstly (adv)	reʃit	רֵאשִׁית
secondly (adv)	ʃenit	שֵׁנִית
thirdly (adv)	ʃliʃit	שְׁלִישִׁית
suddenly (adv)	pit'om	פִּתְאוֹם
at first (in the beginning)	behatslaχa	בַּהַתְחָלָה
for the first time	lariʃona	לָרִאשׁוֹנָה
long before ...	zman rav lifnei ...	זְמַן רַב לִפְנֵי ...
anew (over again)	meχadaʃ	מֵחָדָשׁ
for good (adv)	letamid	לְתָמִיד
never (adv)	af 'pa‘am, me‘olam	מֵעוֹלָם, אַף פַּעַם
again (adv)	ʃuv	שׁוּב
now (adv)	aχʃav, ka‘et	עַכְשָׁיו, כָּעֵת
often (adv)	le‘itim krovot	לְעִיתִּים קְרוֹבוֹת
then (adv)	az	אָז
urgently (quickly)	bidχifut	בִּדְחִיפוּת
usually (adv)	be'dereχ klal	בְּדֶרֶךְ כְּלָל
by the way, ...	'dereχ 'agav	דֶּרֶךְ אַגַּב
possible (that is ~)	efʃari	אֶפְשָׁרִי
probably (adv)	kanir'e	כַּנִּרְאָה
maybe (adv)	ulai	אוּלַי
besides ...	χuts mize ...	חוּץ מִזֶּה ...
that's why ...	laχen	לָכֵן
in spite of ...	lamrot ...	לַמְרוֹת ...
thanks to ...	hodot le...	הוֹדוֹת לְ...
what (pron.)	ma	מַה
that (conj.)	ʃe	שֶׁ
something	'maʃehu	מַשֶּׁהוּ
anything (something)	'maʃehu	מַשֶּׁהוּ
nothing	klum	כְּלוּם

who (pron.)	mi	מִי
someone	'miʃehu, 'miʃehi	מִישֶׁהוּ (ז), מִישֶׁהִי (נ)
somebody	'miʃehu, 'miʃehi	מִישֶׁהוּ (ז), מִישֶׁהִי (נ)
nobody	af eχad, af aχat	אַף אֶחָד (ז), אַף אַחַת (נ)
nowhere (a voyage to ~)	leʃum makom	לְשׁוּם מָקוֹם
nobody's	lo ʃayaχ le'af eχad	לֹא שַׁיָּךְ לְאַף אֶחָד
somebody's	ʃel 'miʃehu	שֶׁל מִישֶׁהוּ
so (I'm ~ glad)	kol kaχ	כָּל־כָּךְ
also (as well)	gam	גַּם
too (as well)	gam	גַּם

6. Function words. Adverbs. Part 2

Why?	ma'du'a?	מַדּוּעַ?
for some reason	miʃum ma	מִשּׁוּם־מָה
because …	miʃum ʃe	מִשּׁוּם שֶׁ
for some purpose	lematara 'kolʃehi	לְמַטָּרָה כָּלְשֶׁהִי
and	ve …	וְ ...
or	o	אוֹ
but	aval, ulam	אֲבָל, אוּלָם
for (e.g., ~ me)	biʃvil	בִּשְׁבִיל
too (~ many people)	yoter midai	יוֹתֵר מִדַּי
only (exclusively)	rak	רַק
exactly (adv)	bediyuk	בְּדִיּוּק
about (more or less)	be''ereχ	בְּעֵרֶךְ
approximately (adv)	be''ereχ	בְּעֵרֶךְ
approximate (adj)	meʃo'ar	מְשׁוֹעָר
almost (adv)	kim'at	כִּמְעַט
the rest	ʃe'ar	שְׁאָר (ז)
the other (second)	aχer	אַחֵר
other (different)	aχer	אַחֵר
each (adj)	kol	כֹּל
any (no matter which)	kolʃehu	כָּלְשֶׁהוּ
many, much (a lot of)	harbe	הַרְבֵּה
many people	harbe	הַרְבֵּה
all (everyone)	kulam	כּוּלָם
in return for …	tmurat …	תְּמוּרַת ...
in exchange (adv)	bitmura	בִּתְמוּרָה
by hand (made)	bayad	בַּיָּד
hardly (negative opinion)	safek im	סָפֵק אִם
probably (adv)	karov levadai	קָרוֹב לְוַדַּאי
on purpose (intentionally)	'davka	דַּוְוקָא

by accident (adv)	bemikre	בְּמִקְרֶה
very (adv)	me'od	מְאוֹד
for example (adv)	lemaʃal	לְמָשָׁל
between	bein	בֵּין
among	be'kerev	בְּקֶרֶב
so much (such a lot)	kol kaχ harbe	כָּל־כָּךְ הַרבֵּה
especially (adv)	bimyuχad	בְּמיוּחָד

NUMBERS. MISCELLANEOUS

7. Cardinal numbers. Part 1

0 zero	'efes	אֶפֶס (ז)
1 one	exad	אֶחָד (ז)
1 one (fem.)	axat	אַחַת (נ)
2 two	'ʃtayim	שְׁתַּיִם (נ)
3 three	ʃaloʃ	שָׁלוֹשׁ (נ)
4 four	arba	אַרְבַּע (נ)
5 five	xameʃ	חָמֵשׁ (נ)
6 six	ʃeʃ	שֵׁשׁ (נ)
7 seven	'ʃeva	שֶׁבַע (נ)
8 eight	'ʃmone	שְׁמוֹנֶה (נ)
9 nine	'teʃa	תֵּשַׁע (נ)
10 ten	'eser	עֶשֶׂר (נ)
11 eleven	axat esre	אַחַת־עֶשְׂרֵה (נ)
12 twelve	ʃteim esre	שְׁתֵּים־עֶשְׂרֵה (נ)
13 thirteen	ʃloʃ esre	שְׁלוֹשׁ־עֶשְׂרֵה (נ)
14 fourteen	arba esre	אַרְבַּע־עֶשְׂרֵה (נ)
15 fifteen	xameʃ esre	חָמֵשׁ־עֶשְׂרֵה (נ)
16 sixteen	ʃeʃ esre	שֵׁשׁ־עֶשְׂרֵה (נ)
17 seventeen	ʃva esre	שְׁבַע־עֶשְׂרֵה (נ)
18 eighteen	ʃmone esre	שְׁמוֹנֶה־עֶשְׂרֵה (נ)
19 nineteen	tʃa esre	תְּשַׁע־עֶשְׂרֵה (נ)
20 twenty	esrim	עֶשְׂרִים
21 twenty-one	esrim ve'exad	עֶשְׂרִים וְאֶחָד
22 twenty-two	esrim u'ʃnayim	עֶשְׂרִים וּשְׁנַיִם
23 twenty-three	esrim uʃloʃa	עֶשְׂרִים וּשְׁלוֹשָׁה
30 thirty	ʃloʃim	שְׁלוֹשִׁים
31 thirty-one	ʃloʃim ve'exad	שְׁלוֹשִׁים וְאֶחָד
32 thirty-two	ʃloʃim u'ʃnayim	שְׁלוֹשִׁים וּשְׁנַיִם
33 thirty-three	ʃloʃim uʃloʃa	שְׁלוֹשִׁים וּשְׁלוֹשָׁה
40 forty	arba'im	אַרְבָּעִים
41 forty-one	arba'im ve'exad	אַרְבָּעִים וְאֶחָד
42 forty-two	arba'im u'ʃnayim	אַרְבָּעִים וּשְׁנַיִם
43 forty-three	arba'im uʃloʃa	אַרְבָּעִים וּשְׁלוֹשָׁה
50 fifty	xamiʃim	חֲמִישִׁים
51 fifty-one	xamiʃim ve'exad	חֲמִישִׁים וְאֶחָד

52 fifty-two	χamiʃim uʃnayim	חֲמִשִּׁים וּשְׁנַיִם
53 fifty-three	χamiʃim uʃloʃa	חֲמִשִּׁים וּשְׁלוֹשָׁה
60 sixty	ʃiʃim	שִׁשִּׁים
61 sixty-one	ʃiʃim ve'eχad	שִׁשִּׁים וְאֶחָד
62 sixty-two	ʃiʃim uʃnayim	שִׁשִּׁים וּשְׁנַיִם
63 sixty-three	ʃiʃim uʃloʃa	שִׁשִּׁים וּשְׁלוֹשָׁה
70 seventy	ʃiv'im	שִׁבְעִים
71 seventy-one	ʃiv'im ve'eχad	שִׁבְעִים וְאֶחָד
72 seventy-two	ʃiv'im uʃnayim	שִׁבְעִים וּשְׁנַיִם
73 seventy-three	ʃiv'im uʃloʃa	שִׁבְעִים וּשְׁלוֹשָׁה
80 eighty	ʃmonim	שְׁמוֹנִים
81 eighty-one	ʃmonim ve'eχad	שְׁמוֹנִים וְאֶחָד
82 eighty-two	ʃmonim uʃnayim	שְׁמוֹנִים וּשְׁנַיִם
83 eighty-three	ʃmonim uʃloʃa	שְׁמוֹנִים וּשְׁלוֹשָׁה
90 ninety	tiʃim	תִּשְׁעִים
91 ninety-one	tiʃim ve'eχad	תִּשְׁעִים וְאֶחָד
92 ninety-two	tiʃim uʃayim	תִּשְׁעִים וּשְׁנַיִם
93 ninety-three	tiʃim uʃloʃa	תִּשְׁעִים וּשְׁלוֹשָׁה

8. Cardinal numbers. Part 2

100 one hundred	'me'a	מֵאָה (נ)
200 two hundred	ma'tayim	מָאתַיִם
300 three hundred	ʃloʃ me'ot	שְׁלוֹשׁ מֵאוֹת (נ)
400 four hundred	arba me'ot	אַרְבַּע מֵאוֹת (נ)
500 five hundred	χameʃ me'ot	חָמֵשׁ מֵאוֹת (נ)
600 six hundred	ʃeʃ me'ot	שֵׁשׁ מֵאוֹת (נ)
700 seven hundred	ʃva me'ot	שְׁבַע מֵאוֹת (נ)
800 eight hundred	ʃmone me'ot	שְׁמוֹנֶה מֵאוֹת (נ)
900 nine hundred	tʃa me'ot	תְּשַׁע מֵאוֹת (נ)
1000 one thousand	'elef	אֶלֶף (ז)
2000 two thousand	al'payim	אַלְפַּיִם (ז)
3000 three thousand	'ʃloʃet alafim	שְׁלוֹשֶׁת אֲלָפִים (ז)
10000 ten thousand	a'seret alafim	עֲשֶׂרֶת אֲלָפִים (ז)
one hundred thousand	'me'a 'elef	מֵאָה אֶלֶף (ז)
million	milyon	מִילְיוֹן (ז)
billion	milyard	מִילְיַארְד (ז)

9. Ordinal numbers

first (adj)	riʃon	רִאשׁוֹן
second (adj)	ʃeni	שֵׁנִי

third (adj)	ʃliʃi	שְׁלִישִׁי
fourth (adj)	revi'i	רְבִיעִי
fifth (adj)	χamiʃi	חֲמִישִׁי
sixth (adj)	ʃiʃi	שִׁישִׁי
seventh (adj)	ʃvi'i	שְׁבִיעִי
eighth (adj)	ʃmini	שְׁמִינִי
ninth (adj)	tʃi'i	תְּשִׁיעִי
tenth (adj)	asiri	עֲשִׂירִי

COLOURS. UNITS OF MEASUREMENT

10. Colors

color	'tseva	צֶבַע (ז)
shade (tint)	gavan	גָוֶון (ז)
hue	gavan	גָוֶון (ז)
rainbow	'keʃet	קֶשֶׁת (נ)
white (adj)	lavan	לָבָן
black (adj)	ʃaxor	שָׁחוֹר
gray (adj)	afor	אָפוֹר
green (adj)	yarok	יָרוֹק
yellow (adj)	tsahov	צָהוֹב
red (adj)	adom	אָדוֹם
blue (adj)	kaxol	כָּחוֹל
light blue (adj)	taxol	תָּכוֹל
pink (adj)	varod	וָרוֹד
orange (adj)	katom	כָּתוֹם
violet (adj)	segol	סָגוֹל
brown (adj)	xum	חוּם
golden (adj)	zahov	זָהוֹב
silvery (adj)	kasuf	כָּסוּף
beige (adj)	beʒ	בֶּז'
cream (adj)	be'tseva krem	בְּצֶבַע קְרֶם
turquoise (adj)	turkiz	טוּרְקִיז
cherry red (adj)	bordo	בּוֹרדוֹ
lilac (adj)	segol	סָגוֹל
crimson (adj)	patol	פָּטוֹל
light (adj)	bahir	בָּהִיר
dark (adj)	kehe	כֵּהֶה
bright, vivid (adj)	bohek	בּוֹהֵק
colored (pencils)	tsiv'oni	צִבְעוֹנִי
color (e.g., ~ film)	tsiv'oni	צִבְעוֹנִי
black-and-white (adj)	ʃaxor lavan	שָׁחוֹר-לָבָן
plain (one-colored)	xad tsiv'i	חַד-צִבְעִי
multicolored (adj)	sasgoni	סַסְגוֹנִי

11. Units of measurement

weight	miʃkal	מִשְׁקָל (ז)
length	'oreχ	אוֹרֶךְ (ז)
width	'roχav	רוֹחַב (ז)
height	'gova	גּוֹבַהּ (ז)
depth	'omek	עוֹמֶק (ז)
volume	'nefaχ	נֶפַח (ז)
area	'ʃetaχ	שֶׁטַח (ז)

gram	gram	גְרָם (ז)
milligram	miligram	מִילִיגְרָם (ז)
kilogram	kilogram	קִילוֹגְרָם (ז)
ton	ton	טוֹן (ז)
pound	'pa'und	פָּאוּנְד (ז)
ounce	'unkiya	אוּנְקִיָה (נ)

meter	'meter	מֶטֶר (ז)
millimeter	mili'meter	מִילִימֶטֶר (ז)
centimeter	senti'meter	סָנְטִימֶטֶר (ז)
kilometer	kilo'meter	קִילוֹמֶטֶר (ז)
mile	mail	מַייל (ז)

inch	intʃ	אִינְצ' (ז)
foot	'regel	רֶגֶל (נ)
yard	yard	יַרְד (ז)

square meter	'meter ra'vu'a	מֶטֶר רָבוּעַ (ז)
hectare	hektar	הֶקְטָר (ז)

liter	litr	לִיטֶר (ז)
degree	ma'ala	מַעֲלָה (נ)
volt	volt	ווֹלְט (ז)
ampere	amper	אַמְפֶּר (ז)
horsepower	'koaχ sus	כּוֹחַ סוּס (ז)

quantity	kamut	כַּמוּת (נ)
a little bit of …	kt͡sat …	קְצָת …
half	'χet͡si	חֲצִי (ז)

dozen	tresar	תְּרֵיסָר (ז)
piece (item)	yeχida	יְחִידָה (נ)

size	'godel	גּוֹדֶל (ז)
scale (map ~)	kne mida	קְנֵה מִידָה (ז)

minimal (adj)	mini'mali	מִינִימָאלִי
the smallest (adj)	hakatan beyoter	הַקָטָן בְּיוֹתֵר
medium (adj)	memut͡sa	מְמוּצָע
maximal (adj)	maksi'mali	מַקְסִימָלִי
the largest (adj)	hagadol beyoter	הַגָדוֹל בְּיוֹתֵר

12. Containers

canning jar (glass ~)	tsin'tsenet	צִנְצֶנֶת (נ)
can	paxit	פַּחִית (נ)
bucket	dli	דְּלִי (ז)
barrel	xavit	חָבִית (נ)
wash basin (e.g., plastic ~)	gigit	גִּיגִית (נ)
tank (100L water ~)	meixal	מֵיכָל (ז)
hip flask	meimiya	מֵימִיָּה (נ)
jerrycan	'dʒerikan	גֶ'רִיקָן (ז)
tank (e.g., tank car)	mexalit	מֵיכָלִית (נ)
mug	'sefel	סֵפֶל (ז)
cup (of coffee, etc.)	'sefel	סֵפֶל (ז)
saucer	taxtit	תַּחְתִּית (נ)
glass (tumbler)	kos	כּוֹס (נ)
wine glass	ga'vi'a	גָּבִיעַ (ז)
stock pot (soup pot)	sir	סִיר (ז)
bottle (~ of wine)	bakbuk	בַּקְבּוּק (ז)
neck (of the bottle, etc.)	tsavar habakbuk	צַוַּאר הַבַּקְבּוּק (ז)
carafe (decanter)	kad	כַּד (ז)
pitcher	kankan	קַנְקַן (ז)
vessel (container)	kli	כְּלִי (ז)
pot (crock, stoneware ~)	sir 'xeres	סִיר חֶרֶס (ז)
vase	agartal	אֲגַרְטָל (ז)
bottle (perfume ~)	tsloxit	צְלוֹחִית (נ)
vial, small bottle	bakbukon	בַּקְבּוּקוֹן (ז)
tube (of toothpaste)	ʃfo'feret	שְׁפוֹפֶרֶת (נ)
sack (bag)	sak	שַׂק (ז)
bag (paper ~, plastic ~)	sakit	שַׂקִּית (נ)
pack (of cigarettes, etc.)	xafisa	חֲפִיסָה (נ)
box (e.g., shoebox)	kufsa	קוּפְסָה (נ)
crate	argaz	אַרְגָּז (ז)
basket	sal	סַל (ז)

MAIN VERBS

13. The most important verbs. Part 1

to advise (vt)	leya'ets	לְיָיעֵץ
to agree (say yes)	lehaskim	לְהַסְכִּים
to answer (vi, vt)	la'anot	לַעֲנוֹת
to apologize (vi)	lehitnatsel	לְהִתְנַצֵּל
to arrive (vi)	leha'gi'a	לְהַגִּיעַ
to ask (~ oneself)	liʃol	לִשְׁאוֹל
to ask (~ sb to do sth)	levakeʃ	לְבַקֵּשׁ
to be (vi)	lihyot	לִהְיוֹת
to be afraid	lefaxed	לְפַחֵד
to be hungry	lihyot ra'ev	לִהְיוֹת רָעֵב
to be interested in ...	lehit'anyen be...	לְהִתְעַנְיֵין בְּ...
to be needed	lehidareʃ	לְהִידָרֵשׁ
to be surprised	lehitpale	לְהִתְפַּלֵא
to be thirsty	lihyot tsame	לִהְיוֹת צָמֵא
to begin (vt)	lehatxil	לְהַתְחִיל
to belong to ...	lehiʃtayex	לְהִשְׁתַּיֵיך
to boast (vi)	lehitravrev	לְהִתְרַבְרֵב
to break (split into pieces)	liʃbor	לִשְׁבּוֹר
to call (~ for help)	likro	לִקְרוֹא
can (v aux)	yaxol	יָכוֹל
to catch (vt)	litfos	לִתְפּוֹס
to change (vt)	leʃanot	לְשַׁנּוֹת
to choose (select)	livxor	לִבְחוֹר
to come down (the stairs)	la'redet	לָרֶדֶת
to compare (vt)	lehaʃvot	לְהַשְׁווֹת
to complain (vi, vt)	lehitlonen	לְהִתְלוֹנֵן
to confuse (mix up)	lehitbalbel	לְהִתְבַּלְבֵּל
to continue (vt)	lehamʃix	לְהַמְשִׁיך
to control (vt)	liʃlot	לִשְׁלוֹט
to cook (dinner)	levaʃel	לְבַשֵּׁל
to cost (vt)	la'alot	לַעֲלוֹת
to count (add up)	lispor	לִסְפּוֹר
to count on ...	lismox al	לִסְמוֹך עַל
to create (vt)	litsor	לִיצוֹר
to cry (weep)	livkot	לִבְכּוֹת

14. The most important verbs. Part 2

to deceive (vi, vt)	leramot	לְרַמּוֹת
to decorate (tree, street)	lekaʃet	לְקַשֵּׁט
to defend (a country, etc.)	lehagen	לְהָגֵן
to demand (request firmly)	lidroʃ	לִדְרוֹשׁ
to dig (vt)	laxpor	לַחְפּוֹר
to discuss (vt)	ladun	לָדוּן
to do (vt)	la'asot	לַעֲשׂוֹת
to doubt (have doubts)	lefakpek	לְפַקְפֵּק
to drop (let fall)	lehapil	לְהַפִּיל
to enter (room, house, etc.)	lehikanes	לְהִכָּנֵס
to excuse (forgive)	lis'loax	לִסְלוֹחַ
to exist (vi)	lehitkayem	לְהִתְקַיֵּם
to expect (foresee)	laxazot	לַחֲזוֹת
to explain (vt)	lehasbir	לְהַסְבִּיר
to fall (vi)	lipol	לִיפּוֹל
to find (vt)	limtso	לִמְצוֹא
to finish (vt)	lesayem	לְסַיֵּם
to fly (vi)	la'uf	לָעוּף
to follow ... (come after)	la'akov axarei	לַעֲקוֹב אַחֲרֵי
to forget (vi, vt)	liʃkoax	לִשְׁכּוֹחַ
to forgive (vt)	lis'loax	לִסְלוֹחַ
to give (vt)	latet	לָתֵת
to give a hint	lirmoz	לִרְמוֹז
to go (on foot)	la'lexet	לָלֶכֶת
to go for a swim	lehitraxets	לְהִתְרַחֵץ
to go out (for dinner, etc.)	latset	לָצֵאת
to guess (the answer)	lenaxeʃ	לְנַחֵשׁ
to have (vt)	lehaxzik	לְהַחְזִיק
to have breakfast	le'exol aruxat 'boker	לָאֱכוֹל אֲרוּחַת בּוֹקֶר
to have dinner	le'exol aruxat 'erev	לָאֱכוֹל אֲרוּחַת עֶרֶב
to have lunch	le'exol aruxat tsaha'rayim	לָאֱכוֹל אֲרוּחַת צָהֳרַיִם
to hear (vt)	liʃmo'a	לִשְׁמוֹעַ
to help (vt)	la'azor	לַעֲזוֹר
to hide (vt)	lehastir	לְהַסְתִּיר
to hope (vi, vt)	lekavot	לְקַוּוֹת
to hunt (vi, vt)	latsud	לָצוּד
to hurry (vi)	lemaher	לְמַהֵר

15. The most important verbs. Part 3

to inform (vt)	leho'dia	לְהוֹדִיעַ
to insist (vi, vt)	lehit'akeʃ	לְהִתְעַקֵּש
to insult (vt)	leha'aliv	לְהַעֲלִיב
to invite (vt)	lehazmin	לְהַזְמִין
to joke (vi)	lehitba'deaχ	לְהִתְבַּדֵּחַ
to keep (vt)	liʃmor	לִשְמוֹר
to keep silent	liʃtok	לִשְתּוֹק
to kill (vt)	laharog	לַהֲרוֹג
to know (sb)	lehakir et	לְהַכִּיר אֶת
to know (sth)	la'da'at	לָדַעַת
to laugh (vi)	liʦχok	לִצְחוֹק
to liberate (city, etc.)	leʃaχrer	לְשַחְרֵר
to like (I like …)	limʦo χen be'ei'nayim	לִמְצוֹא חֵן בְּעֵינַיִים
to look for … (search)	leχapes	לְחַפֵּש
to love (sb)	le'ehov	לֶאֱהוֹב
to make a mistake	lit'ot	לִטְעוֹת
to manage, to run	lenahel	לְנַהֵל
to mean (signify)	lomar	לוֹמַר
to mention (talk about)	lehazkir	לְהַזְכִּיר
to miss (school, etc.)	lehaχsir	לְהַחְסִיר
to notice (see)	lasim lev	לָשִים לֵב
to object (vi, vt)	lehitnaged	לְהִתְנַגֵּד
to observe (see)	liʦpot, lehaʃkif	לִצְפּוֹת, לְהַשְקִיף
to open (vt)	lif'toaχ	לִפְתּוֹחַ
to order (meal, etc.)	lehazmin	לְהַזְמִין
to order (mil.)	lifkod	לִפְקוֹד
to own (possess)	lihyot 'ba'al ʃel	לִהְיוֹת בַּעַל שֶל
to participate (vi)	lehiʃtatef	לְהִשְתַּתֵּף
to pay (vi, vt)	leʃalem	לְשַלֵם
to permit (vt)	leharʃot	לְהַרְשוֹת
to plan (vt)	letaχnen	לְתַכְנֵן
to play (children)	lesaχek	לְשַׂחֵק
to pray (vi, vt)	lehitpalel	לְהִתְפַּלֵל
to prefer (vt)	leha'adif	לְהַעֲדִיף
to promise (vt)	lehav'tiaχ	לְהַבְטִיחַ
to pronounce (vt)	levate	לְבַטֵא
to propose (vt)	leha'ʦi'a	לְהַצִּיעַ
to punish (vt)	leha'aniʃ	לְהַעֲנִיש

16. The most important verbs. Part 4

to read (vi, vt)	likro	לִקְרוֹא
to recommend (vt)	lehamliʦ	לְהַמְלִיץ

to refuse (vi, vt)	lesarev	לְסָרֵב
to regret (be sorry)	lehitsta'er	לְהִצְטַעֵר
to rent (sth from sb)	liskor	לִשְׂכּוֹר
to repeat (say again)	laχazor al	לַחְזוֹר עַל
to reserve, to book	lehazmin meroʃ	לְהַזְמִין מֵרֹאשׁ
to run (vi)	laruts	לָרוּץ
to save (rescue)	lehatsil	לְהַצִּיל
to say (~ thank you)	lomar	לוֹמַר
to scold (vt)	linzof	לִנְזוֹף
to see (vt)	lir'ot	לִרְאוֹת
to sell (vt)	limkor	לִמְכּוֹר
to send (vt)	liʃ'loaχ	לִשְׁלוֹחַ
to shoot (vi)	lirot	לִירוֹת
to shout (vi)	lits'ok	לִצְעוֹק
to show (vt)	lehar'ot	לְהַרְאוֹת
to sign (document)	laχtom	לַחְתּוֹם
to sit down (vi)	lehityaʃev	לְהִתְיַישֵׁב
to smile (vi)	leχayeχ	לְחַיֵּיךְ
to speak (vi, vt)	ledaber	לְדַבֵּר
to steal (money, etc.)	lignov	לִגְנוֹב
to stop (for pause, etc.)	la'atsor	לַעֲצוֹר
to stop (please ~ calling me)	lehafsik	לְהַפְסִיק
to study (vt)	lilmod	לִלְמוֹד
to swim (vi)	lisχot	לִשְׂחוֹת
to take (vt)	la'kaχat	לָקַחַת
to think (vi, vt)	laχʃov	לַחְשׁוֹב
to threaten (vt)	le'ayem	לְאַיֵּים
to touch (with hands)	la'ga'at	לָגַעַת
to translate (vt)	letargem	לְתַרְגֵּם
to trust (vt)	liv'toaχ	לִבְטוֹחַ
to try (attempt)	lenasot	לְנַסּוֹת
to turn (e.g., ~ left)	lifnot	לִפְנוֹת
to underestimate (vt)	leham'it be''ereχ	לְהַמְעִיט בְּעֶרְךָ
to understand (vt)	lehavin	לְהָבִין
to unite (vt)	le'aχed	לְאַחֵד
to wait (vt)	lehamtin	לְהַמְתִּין
to want (wish, desire)	lirtsot	לִרְצוֹת
to warn (vt)	lehazhir	לְהַזְהִיר
to work (vi)	la'avod	לַעֲבוֹד
to write (vt)	liχtov	לִכְתּוֹב
to write down	lirʃom	לִרְשׁוֹם

TIME. CALENDAR

17. Weekdays

Monday	yom ʃeni	יוֹם שֵׁנִי (ז)
Tuesday	yom ʃliʃi	יוֹם שְׁלִישִׁי (ז)
Wednesday	yom revi'i	יוֹם רְבִיעִי (ז)
Thursday	yom xamiʃi	יוֹם חֲמִישִׁי (ז)
Friday	yom ʃiʃi	יוֹם שִׁישִׁי (ז)
Saturday	ʃabat	שַׁבָּת (נ)
Sunday	yom riʃon	יוֹם רִאשׁוֹן (ז)

today (adv)	hayom	הַיּוֹם
tomorrow (adv)	maxar	מָחָר
the day after tomorrow	maxara'tayim	מָחֳרָתַיִם
yesterday (adv)	etmol	אֶתְמוֹל
the day before yesterday	ʃilʃom	שִׁלְשׁוֹם

day	yom	יוֹם (ז)
working day	yom avoda	יוֹם עֲבוֹדָה (ז)
public holiday	yom xag	יוֹם חַג (ז)
day off	yom menuxa	יוֹם מְנוּחָה (ז)
weekend	sof ʃa'vu'a	סוֹף שָׁבוּעַ

all day long	kol hayom	כָּל הַיּוֹם
the next day (adv)	lamaxarat	לַמָּחֳרָת
two days ago	lifnei yo'mayim	לִפְנֵי יוֹמַיִים
the day before	'erev	עֶרֶב
daily (adj)	yomyomi	יוֹמִיוֹמִי
every day (adv)	midei yom	מִדֵּי יוֹם

week	ʃa'vua	שָׁבוּעַ (ז)
last week (adv)	baʃa'vu'a ʃe'avar	בַּשָּׁבוּעַ שֶׁעָבַר
next week (adv)	baʃa'vu'a haba	בַּשָּׁבוּעַ הַבָּא
weekly (adj)	ʃvu'i	שְׁבוּעִי
every week (adv)	kol ʃa'vu'a	כָּל שָׁבוּעַ
twice a week	pa'a'mayim beʃa'vu'a	פַּעֲמַיִים בְּשָׁבוּעַ
every Tuesday	kol yom ʃliʃi	כָּל יוֹם שְׁלִישִׁי

18. Hours. Day and night

morning	'boker	בּוֹקֶר (ז)
in the morning	ba'boker	בַּבּוֹקֶר
noon, midday	tsaha'rayim	צָהֳרַיִים (ז"ר)

in the afternoon	axar hatsaha'rayim	אַחַר הַצָּהֳרַיִם
evening	'erev	עֶרֶב (ז)
in the evening	ba''erev	בָּעֶרֶב
night	'laila	לַילָה (ז)
at night	ba'laila	בַּלַּילָה
midnight	xatsot	חֲצוֹת (נ)
second	ʃniya	שְׁנִיָּה (נ)
minute	daka	דַּקָּה (נ)
hour	ʃa'a	שָׁעָה (נ)
half an hour	xatsi ʃa'a	חֲצִי שָׁעָה (נ)
a quarter-hour	'reva ʃa'a	רֶבַע שָׁעָה (ז)
fifteen minutes	xameʃ esre dakot	חָמֵשׁ עֶשֹׂרֵה דַקוֹת
24 hours	yemama	יְמָמָה (נ)
sunrise	zrixa	זְרִיחָה (נ)
dawn	'ʃaxar	שַׁחַר (ז)
early morning	'ʃaxar	שַׁחַר (ז)
sunset	ʃki'a	שְׁקִיעָה (נ)
early in the morning	mukdam ba'boker	מוּקְדָּם בַּבּוֹקֶר
this morning	ha'boker	הַבּוֹקֶר
tomorrow morning	maxar ba'boker	מָחָר בַּבּוֹקֶר
this afternoon	hayom axarei hatsaha'rayim	הַיּוֹם אַחֲרֵי הַצָּהֳרַיִם
in the afternoon	axar hatsaha'rayim	אַחַר הַצָּהֳרַיִם
tomorrow afternoon	maxar axarei hatsaha'rayim	מָחָר אַחֲרֵי הַצָּהֳרַיִם
tonight (this evening)	ha''erev	הָעֶרֶב
tomorrow night	maxar ba''erev	מָחָר בָּעֶרֶב
at 3 o'clock sharp	baʃa'a ʃaloʃ bediyuk	בְּשָׁעָה שָׁלוֹשׁ בְּדִיּוּק
about 4 o'clock	bisvivot arba	בִּסְבִיבוֹת אַרְבַּע
by 12 o'clock	ad ʃteim esre	עַד שְׁתֵּים־עֶשֹׂרֵה
in 20 minutes	be'od esrim dakot	בְּעוֹד עֶשֹׂרִים דַקוֹת
in an hour	be'od ʃa'a	בְּעוֹד שָׁעָה
on time (adv)	bazman	בַּזְּמַן
a quarter of ...	'reva le...	רֶבַע לְ...
within an hour	tox ʃa'a	תּוֹךְ שָׁעָה
every 15 minutes	kol 'reva ʃa'a	כָּל רֶבַע שָׁעָה
round the clock	misaviv laʃa'on	מִסָּבִיב לַשָּׁעוֹן

19. Months. Seasons

January	'yanu'ar	יָנוּאָר (ז)
February	'febru'ar	פֶבְּרוּאָר (ז)

March	merts	מָרְץ (ז)
April	april	אַפְּרִיל (ז)
May	mai	מַאי (ז)
June	'yuni	יוּנִי (ז)
July	'yuli	יוּלִי (ז)
August	'ogust	אוֹגוּסְט (ז)
September	sep'tember	סֶפְּטֶמְבָּר (ז)
October	ok'tober	אוֹקְטוֹבָּר (ז)
November	no'vember	נוֹבֶמְבָּר (ז)
December	de'tsember	דֶצֶמְבָּר (ז)
spring	aviv	אָבִיב (ז)
in spring	ba'aviv	בָּאָבִיב
spring (as adj)	avivi	אָבִיבִי
summer	'kayits	קַיִץ (ז)
in summer	ba'kayits	בַּקַיִץ
summer (as adj)	ketsi	קֵיצִי
fall	stav	סְתָיו (ז)
in fall	bestav	בְּסְתָיו
fall (as adj)	stavi	סְתָווִי
winter	'χoref	חוֹרֶף (ז)
in winter	ba'χoref	בַּחוֹרֶף
winter (as adj)	χorpi	חוֹרְפִּי
month	'χodeʃ	חוֹדֶש (ז)
this month	ha'χodeʃ	הַחוֹדֶש
next month	ba'χodeʃ haba	בַּחוֹדֶש הַבָּא
last month	ba'χodeʃ ʃe'avar	בַּחוֹדֶש שֶׁעָבָר
a month ago	lifnei 'χodeʃ	לִפְנֵי חוֹדֶש
in a month (a month later)	be'od 'χodeʃ	בְּעוֹד חוֹדֶש
in 2 months (2 months later)	be'od χod'ʃayim	בְּעוֹד חוֹדְשַׁיים
the whole month	kol ha'χodeʃ	כָּל הַחוֹדֶש
all month long	kol ha'χodeʃ	כָּל הַחוֹדֶש
monthly (~ magazine)	χodʃi	חוֹדְשִׁי
monthly (adv)	χodʃit	חוֹדְשִׁית
every month	kol 'χodeʃ	כָּל חוֹדֶש
twice a month	pa'a'mayim be'χodeʃ	פַּעֲמַיים בְּחוֹדֶש
year	ʃana	שָׁנָה (נ)
this year	haʃana	הַשָּׁנָה
next year	baʃana haba'a	בַּשָּׁנָה הַבָּאָה
last year	baʃana ʃe'avra	בַּשָּׁנָה שֶׁעָבְרָה
a year ago	lifnei ʃana	לִפְנֵי שָׁנָה
in a year	be'od ʃana	בְּעוֹד שָׁנָה

in two years	be'od ʃna'tayim	בְּעוֹד שְׁנָתַיים
the whole year	kol haʃana	כָּל הַשָׁנָה
all year long	kol haʃana	כָּל הַשָׁנָה
every year	kol ʃana	כָּל שָׁנָה
annual (adj)	ʃnati	שְׁנָתִי
annually (adv)	midei ʃana	מִדֵי שָׁנָה
4 times a year	arba pa'amim be'xodeʃ	אַרְבַּע פְּעָמִים בְּחוֹדָש
date (e.g., today's ~)	ta'arix	תַאֲרִיך (ז)
date (e.g., ~ of birth)	ta'arix	תַאֲרִיך (ז)
calendar	'luax ʃana	לוֹחַ שָׁנָה (ז)
half a year	xatsi ʃana	חֲצִי שָׁנָה (ז)
six months	ʃiʃa xodaʃim, xatsi ʃana	חֲצִי שָׁנָה, שִׁישָׁה חוֹדָשִׁים
season (summer, etc.)	ona	עוֹנָה (נ)
century	'me'a	מָאָה (נ)

TRAVEL. HOTEL

20. Trip. Travel

tourism, travel	tayarut	תַּיָּירוּת (נ)
tourist	tayar	תַּיָּיר (ז)
trip, voyage	tiyul	טִיוּל (ז)
adventure	harpatka	הַרְפַּתְקָה (נ)
trip, journey	nesi'a	נְסִיעָה (נ)
vacation	χuffa	חוּפְשָׁה (נ)
to be on vacation	lihyot beχuffa	לִהְיוֹת בְּחוּפְשָׁה
rest	menuχa	מְנוּחָה (נ)
train	ra'kevet	רַכֶּבֶת (נ)
by train	bera'kevet	בְּרַכֶּבֶת
airplane	matos	מָטוֹס (ז)
by airplane	bematos	בְּמָטוֹס
by car	bemeχonit	בִּמְכוֹנִית
by ship	be'oniya	בָּאוֹנִיָּיה
luggage	mit'an	מִטְעָן (ז)
suitcase	mizvada	מִזְוָוֹדָה (נ)
luggage cart	eglat mit'an	עֲגָלַת מִטְעָן (נ)
passport	darkon	דַּרְכּוֹן (ז)
visa	'viza, affra	וִיזָה, אַשְׁרָה (נ)
ticket	kartis	כַּרְטִיס (ז)
air ticket	kartis tisa	כַּרְטִיס טִיסָה (ז)
guidebook	madriχ	מַדְרִיךְ (ז)
map (tourist ~)	mapa	מַפָּה (נ)
area (rural ~)	ezor	אֵזוֹר (ז)
place, site	makom	מָקוֹם (ז)
exotica (n)	ek'zotika	אֶקְזוֹטִיקָה (נ)
exotic (adj)	ek'zoti	אֶקְזוֹטִי
amazing (adj)	nifla	נִפְלָא
group	kvutsa	קְבוּצָה (נ)
excursion, sightseeing tour	tiyul	טִיוּל (ז)
guide (person)	madriχ tiyulim	מַדְרִיךְ טִיּוּלִים (ז)

21. Hotel

hotel	malon	מָלוֹן (ז)
motel	motel	מוֹטֶל (ז)
three-star (~ hotel)	ʃloʃa koχavim	שְׁלוֹשָׁה כּוֹכָבִים
five-star	χamiʃa koχavim	חֲמִישָׁה כּוֹכָבִים
to stay (in a hotel, etc.)	lehit'aχsen	לְהִתְאַכְסֵן
room	'χeder	חֶדֶר (ז)
single room	'χeder yaχid	חֶדֶר יָחִיד (ז)
double room	'χeder zugi	חֶדֶר זוּגִי (ז)
to book a room	lehazmin 'χeder	לְהַזְמִין חֶדֶר
half board	χatsi pensiyon	חֲצִי פֶּנְסִיוֹן (ז)
full board	pensyon male	פֶּנְסִיוֹן מָלֵא (ז)
with bath	im am'batya	עִם אַמְבַּטְיָה
with shower	im mik'laχat	עִם מִקְלַחַת
satellite television	tele'vizya bekvalim	טֶלֶוִוִיזְיָה בְּכְבָלִים (נ)
air-conditioner	mazgan	מַזְגָן (ז)
towel	ma'gevet	מַגֶבֶת (נ)
key	maf'teaχ	מַפְתֵחַ (ז)
administrator	amarkal	אֲמַרְכָּל (ז)
chambermaid	χadranit	חַדְרָנִית (נ)
porter, bellboy	sabal	סַבָּל (ז)
doorman	pakid kabala	פְּקִיד קַבָּלָה (ז)
restaurant	mis'ada	מִסְעָדָה (נ)
pub, bar	bar	בָּר (ז)
breakfast	aruχat 'boker	אֲרוּחַת בּוֹקֶר (נ)
dinner	aruχat 'erev	אֲרוּחַת עֶרֶב (נ)
buffet	miznon	מִזְנוֹן (ז)
lobby	'lobi	לוֹבִּי (ז)
elevator	ma'alit	מַעֲלִית (נ)
DO NOT DISTURB	lo lehaf'ri‘a	לֹא לְהַפְרִיעַ
NO SMOKING	asur le'aʃen!	אָסוּר לְעַשֵׁן!

22. Sightseeing

monument	an'darta	אַנְדַרְטָה (נ)
fortress	mivtsar	מִבְצָר (ז)
palace	armon	אַרְמוֹן (ז)
castle	tira	טִירָה (נ)
tower	migdal	מִגְדָל (ז)
mausoleum	ma'uzo'le'um	מָאוּזוֹלֵיאוּם (ז)

architecture	adrixalut	אַדְרִיכָלוּת (נ)
medieval (adj)	benaimi	בֵּינַיימִי
ancient (adj)	atik	עָתִיק
national (adj)	le'umi	לְאוֹמִי
famous (monument, etc.)	mefursam	מְפוֹרסָם

tourist	tayar	תַייָר (ז)
guide (person)	madrix tiyulim	מַדרִיך טִיוּלִים (ז)
excursion, sightseeing tour	tiyul	טִיוּל (ז)
to show (vt)	lehar'ot	לְהַראוֹת
to tell (vt)	lesaper	לְסַפֵּר

to find (vt)	limtso	לִמצוֹא
to get lost (lose one's way)	la'lexet le'ibud	לָלֶכֶת לְאִיבּוּד
map (e.g., subway ~)	mapa	מַפָּה (נ)
map (e.g., city ~)	tarʃim	תַרשִים (ז)

souvenir, gift	maz'keret	מַזכֶּרֶת (נ)
gift shop	xanut matanot	חֲנוּת מַתָנוֹת (נ)
to take pictures	letsalem	לְצַלֵם
to have one's picture taken	lehitstalem	לְהִצטַלֵם

TRANSPORTATION

23. Airport

airport	nemal te'ufa	נְמַל תְּעוּפָה (ז)
airplane	matos	מָטוֹס (ז)
airline	xevrat te'ufa	חֶבְרַת תְּעוּפָה (נ)
air traffic controller	bakar tisa	בַּקָּר טִיסָה (ז)
departure	hamra'a	הַמְרָאָה (נ)
arrival	nexita	נְחִיתָה (נ)
to arrive (by plane)	leha'gi'a betisa	לְהַגִּיעַ בְּטִיסָה
departure time	zman hamra'a	זְמַן הַמְרָאָה (ז)
arrival time	zman nexita	זְמַן נְחִיתָה (ז)
to be delayed	lehit'akev	לְהִתְעַכֵּב
flight delay	ikuv hatisa	עִיכּוּב הַטִּיסָה (ז)
information board	'luax meida	לוּחַ מֵידָע (ז)
information	meida	מֵידָע (ז)
to announce (vt)	leho'dia	לְהוֹדִיעַ
flight (e.g., next ~)	tisa	טִיסָה (נ)
customs	'mexes	מֶכֶס (ז)
customs officer	pakid 'mexes	פְּקִיד מֶכֶס (ז)
customs declaration	hatsharat mexes	הַצְהָרַת מֶכֶס (נ)
to fill out (vt)	lemale	לְמַלֵּא
to fill out the declaration	lemale 'tofes hatshara	לְמַלֵּא טוֹפֶס הַצְהָרָה
passport control	bdikat darkonim	בְּדִיקַת דַּרְכּוֹנִים (נ)
luggage	kvuda	כְּבוּדָה (נ)
hand luggage	kvudat yad	כְּבוּדַת יָד (נ)
luggage cart	eglat kvuda	עֶגְלַת כְּבוּדָה (נ)
landing	nexita	נְחִיתָה (נ)
landing strip	maslul nexita	מַסְלוּל נְחִיתָה (ז)
to land (vi)	linxot	לִנְחוֹת
airstairs	'kevef	כֶּבֶשׁ (ז)
check-in	tfek in	צֶ׳ק אִין (ז)
check-in counter	dalpak tfek in	דַּלְפָּק צֶ׳ק אִין (ז)
to check-in (vi)	leva'tse'a tfek in	לְבַצֵּעַ צֶ׳ק אִין
boarding pass	kartis aliya lematos	כַּרְטִיס עֲלִיָּה לְמָטוֹס (ז)
departure gate	'fa'ar yetsi'a	שַׁעַר יְצִיאָה (ז)

transit	ma'avar	מַעֲבָר (ז)
to wait (vi)	lehamtin	לְהַמְתִּין
departure lounge	traklin tisa	טְרַקְלִין טִיסָה (ז)
to see off	lelavot	לְלַוּוֹת
to say goodbye	lomar lehitra'ot	לוֹמַר לְהִתְרָאוֹת

24. Airplane

airplane	matos	מָטוֹס (ז)
air ticket	kartis tisa	כַּרְטִיס טִיסָה (ז)
airline	xevrat te'ufa	חֶבְרַת תְּעוּפָה (נ)
airport	nemal te'ufa	נְמַל תְּעוּפָה (ז)
supersonic (adj)	al koli	עַל קוֹלִי
captain	kabarnit	קַבַּרְנִיט (ז)
crew	'tsevet	צֶוֶות (ז)
pilot	tayas	טַיָּיס (ז)
flight attendant (fem.)	da'yelet	דַיֶּילֶת (נ)
navigator	navat	נַוָּוט (ז)
wings	kna'fayim	כְּנָפַיִים (נ״ר)
tail	zanav	זָנָב (ז)
cockpit	'kokpit	קוֹקְפִּיט (ז)
engine	ma'no'a	מָנוֹעַ (ז)
undercarriage (landing gear)	kan nesi'a	כַּן נְסִיעָה (ז)
turbine	tur'bina	טוּרבִּינָה (נ)
propeller	madxef	מַדְחֵף (ז)
black box	kufsa ʃxora	קוּפְסָה שְׁחוֹרָה (נ)
yoke (control column)	'hege	הֶגֶה (ז)
fuel	'delek	דֶלֶק (ז)
safety card	hora'ot betixut	הוֹרָאוֹת בְּטִיחוּת (נ״ר)
oxygen mask	masexat xamtsan	מַסֵּיכַת חַמְצָן (נ)
uniform	madim	מַדִים (ז״ר)
life vest	xagorat hatsala	חֲגוֹרַת הַצָּלָה (נ)
parachute	mitsnax	מִצְנָח (ז)
takeoff	hamra'a	הַמְרָאָה (נ)
to take off (vi)	lehamri	לְהַמְרִיא
runway	maslul hamra'a	מַסְלוּל הַמְרָאָה (ז)
visibility	re'ut	רְאוּת (נ)
flight (act of flying)	tisa	טִיסָה (נ)
altitude	'gova	גוֹבַה (ז)
air pocket	kis avir	כִּיס אֲוִויר (ז)
seat	moʃav	מוֹשָׁב (ז)
headphones	ozniyot	אוֹזְנִיּוֹת (נ״ר)

folding tray (tray table)	magaʃ mitkapel	מַגָּשׁ מְתקַפֵּל (ז)
airplane window	tsohar	צוֹהַר (ז)
aisle	ma'avar	מַעֲבָר (ז)

25. Train

train	ra'kevet	רַכֶּבֶת (נ)
commuter train	ra'kevet parvarim	רַכֶּבֶת פַּרבָרִים (נ)
express train	ra'kevet mehira	רַכֶּבֶת מְהִירָה (נ)
diesel locomotive	katar 'dizel	קַטָּר דִיזֶל (ז)
steam locomotive	katar	קַטָּר (ז)

| passenger car | karon | קָרוֹן (ז) |
| dining car | kron mis'ada | קָרוֹן מִסעָדָה (ז) |

rails	mesilot	מְסִילוֹת (נ"ר)
railroad	mesilat barzel	מְסִילַת בַּרזֶל (נ)
railway tie	'eden	אֶדֶן (ז)

platform (railway ~)	ratsif	רָצִיף (ז)
track (~ 1, 2, etc.)	mesila	מְסִילָה (נ)
semaphore	ramzor	רַמזוֹר (ז)
station	taxana	תַּחֲנָה (נ)

engineer (train driver)	nahag ra'kevet	נֶהָג רַכֶּבֶת (ז)
porter (of luggage)	sabal	סַבָּל (ז)
car attendant	sadran ra'kevet	סַדרָן רַכֶּבֶת (ז)
passenger	no'se'a	נוֹסֵעַ (ז)
conductor (ticket inspector)	bodek	בּוֹדֵק (ז)

| corridor (in train) | prozdor | פּרוֹזדוֹר (ז) |
| emergency brake | ma'atsar xirum | מַעֲצָר חִירוּם (ז) |

compartment	ta	תָּא (ז)
berth	dargaʃ	דַרגָשׁ (ז)
upper berth	dargaʃ elyon	דַרגָשׁ עֶליוֹן (ז)
lower berth	dargaʃ taxton	דַרגָשׁ תַּחתּוֹן (ז)
bed linen, bedding	matsa'im	מַצָּעִים (ז"ר)

ticket	kartis	כַּרטִיס (ז)
schedule	'luax zmanim	לוּחַ זמַנִים (ז)
information display	'ʃelet meida	שֶׁלֶט מֵידָע (ז)

to leave, to depart	latset	לָצֵאת
departure (of train)	yetsi'a	יְצִיאָה (נ)
to arrive (ab. train)	leha'gi'a	לְהַגִּיעַ
arrival	haga'a	הַגָּעָה (נ)
to arrive by train	leha'gi'a bera'kevet	לְהַגִּיעַ בְּרַכֶּבֶת
to get on the train	la'alot lera'kevet	לַעֲלוֹת לְכַכֶּבֶת

to get off the train	la'redet mehara'kevet	לָרֶדֶת מֵהַכַּבֶּת
train wreck	hitraskut	הִתְרַסְקוּת (נ)
to derail (vi)	la'redet mipasei ra'kevet	לָרֶדֶת מִפַּסֵי כַּבֶּת
steam locomotive	katar	קַטָר (ז)
stoker, fireman	masik	מַסִיק (ז)
firebox	kivʃan	כִּבשָׁן (ז)
coal	peχam	פֶּחָם (ז)

26. Ship

ship	sfina	סְפִינָה (נ)
vessel	sfina	סְפִינָה (נ)
steamship	oniyat kitor	אוֹנִיַית קִיטוֹר (נ)
riverboat	sfinat nahar	סְפִינַת נָהָר (נ)
cruise ship	oniyat ta'anugot	אוֹנִיַית תַעֲנוּגוֹת (נ)
cruiser	sa'yeret	סַיֶירֶת (נ)
yacht	'yaχta	יַבטָה (נ)
tugboat	go'reret	גוֹרֶרֶת (נ)
barge	arba	אַרבָּה (נ)
ferry	ma'a'boret	מַעֲבּוֹרֶת (נ)
sailing ship	sfinat mifras	סְפִינַת מִפרָשׂ (נ)
brigantine	briganit	בְּרִיגָנִית (נ)
ice breaker	ʃo'veret 'keraχ	שׁוֹבֶרֶת קֶרַח (נ)
submarine	tso'lelet	צוֹלֶלֶת (נ)
boat (flat-bottomed ~)	sira	סִירָה (נ)
dinghy	sira	סִירָה (נ)
lifeboat	sirat hatsala	סִירַת הַצָלָה (נ)
motorboat	sirat ma'no'a	סִירַת מָנוֹעַ (נ)
captain	rav χovel	רַב־חוֹבֵל (ז)
seaman	malaχ	מַלָח (ז)
sailor	yamai	יַמַאי (ז)
crew	'tsevet	צֶוֶות (ז)
boatswain	rav malaχim	רַב־מַלָחִים (ז)
ship's boy	'na'ar sipun	נַעַר סִיפּוּן (ז)
cook	tabaχ	טַבָּח (ז)
ship's doctor	rofe ha'oniya	רוֹפֵא הָאוֹנִיָיה (ז)
deck	sipun	סִיפּוּן (ז)
mast	'toren	תוֹכֶן (ז)
sail	mifras	מִפרָשׂ (ז)
hold	'beten oniya	בֶּטֶן אוֹנִיָיה (נ)
bow (prow)	χartom	חַרטוֹם (ז)

stern	yarketei hasfina	יַרכְּתֵי הַסְפִינָה (זי״ר)
oar	maʃot	מָשׁוֹט (ז)
screw propeller	madχef	מַדחֵף (ז)
cabin	ta	תָּא (ז)
wardroom	mo'adon ktsinim	מוֹעֲדוֹן קְצִינִים (ז)
engine room	χadar meχonot	חֲדַר מְכוֹנוֹת (ז)
bridge	'geʃer hapikud	גֶּשֶׁר הַפִּיקוּד (ז)
radio room	ta alχutan	תָּא אַלחוּטָן (ז)
wave (radio)	'teder	תֶּדֶר (ז)
logbook	yoman ha'oniya	יוֹמַן הָאוֹנִיָּה (ז)
spyglass	miʃ'kefet	מִשׁקֶפֶת (נ)
bell	pa'amon	פַּעֲמוֹן (ז)
flag	'degel	דֶּגֶל (ז)
hawser (mooring ~)	avot ha'oniya	עֲבוֹת הָאוֹנִיָּה (נ)
knot (bowline, etc.)	'keʃer	קֶשֶׁר (ז)
deckrails	ma'ake hasipun	מַעֲקֵה הַסִּיפּוּן (ז)
gangway	'keveʃ	כֶּבֶשׁ (ז)
anchor	'ogen	עוֹגֶן (ז)
to weigh anchor	leharim 'ogen	לְהָרִים עוֹגֶן
to drop anchor	la'agon	לַעֲגּוֹן
anchor chain	ʃar'ʃeret ha'ogen	שַׁרשֶׁרֶת הָעוֹגֶן (נ)
port (harbor)	namal	נָמֵל (ז)
quay, wharf	'mezaχ	מֶזַח (ז)
to berth (moor)	la'agon	לַעֲגּוֹן
to cast off	lehaflig	לְהַפלִיג
trip, voyage	masa, tiyul	מַסָּע (ז), טִיּוּל (ז)
cruise (sea trip)	'ʃayit	שַׁיִט (ז)
course (route)	kivun	כִּיווּן (ז)
route (itinerary)	nativ	נָתִיב (ז)
fairway (safe water channel)	nativ 'ʃayit	נְתִיב שַׁיִט (ז)
shallows	sirton	שִׂרטוֹן (ז)
to run aground	la'alot al hasirton	לַעֲלוֹת עַל הַשִּׂרטוֹן
storm	sufa	סוּפָה (נ)
signal	ot	אוֹת (ז)
to sink (vi)	lit'bo'a	לִטבּוֹעַ
Man overboard!	adam ba'mayim!	אָדָם בַּמַּיִם!
SOS (distress signal)	kri'at hatsala	קְרִיאַת הַצָּלָה
ring buoy	galgal hatsala	גַּלגַּל הַצָּלָה (ז)

CITY

27. Urban transportation

bus	'otobus	אוֹטוֹבּוּס (ז)
streetcar	ra'kevet kala	רַכֶּבֶת קַלָּה (נ)
trolley bus	tro'leibus	טרוֹלֵייבּוּס (ז)
route (of bus, etc.)	maslul	מַסלוּל (ז)
number (e.g., bus ~)	mispar	מִספָּר (ז)
to go by …	lin'so'a be…	לִנסוֹעַ בְּ...
to get on (~ the bus)	la'alot	לַעֲלוֹת
to get off …	la'redet mi…	לָרֶדֶת מִ...
stop (e.g., bus ~)	taχana	תַחֲנָה (נ)
next stop	hataχana haba'a	הַתַחֲנָה הַבָּאָה (נ)
terminus	hataχana ha'aχrona	הַתַחֲנָה הָאַחרוֹנָה (נ)
schedule	'luaχ zmanim	לוּחַ זמַנִים (ז)
to wait (vt)	lehamtin	לְהַמתִין
ticket	kartis	כַּרטִיס (ז)
fare	meχir hanesiya	מְחִיר הַנְסִיעָה (ז)
cashier (ticket seller)	kupai	קוּפַּאי (ז)
ticket inspection	bi'koret kartisim	בִּיקוֹרֶת כַּרטִיסִים (נ)
ticket inspector	mevaker	מְבַקֵר (ז)
to be late (for …)	le'aχer	לְאַחֵר
to miss (~ the train, etc.)	lefasfes	לְפַסְפֵּס
to be in a hurry	lemaher	לְמַהֵר
taxi, cab	monit	מוֹנִית (נ)
taxi driver	nahag monit	נָהַג מוֹנִית (ז)
by taxi	bemonit	בְּמוֹנִית
taxi stand	taχanat moniyot	תַחֲנַת מוֹנִיוֹת (נ)
to call a taxi	lehazmin monit	לְהַזמִין מוֹנִית
to take a taxi	la'kaχat monit	לָקַחַת מוֹנִית
traffic	tnu'a	תנוּעָה (נ)
traffic jam	pkak	פּקָק (ז)
rush hour	ʃa'ot 'omes	שְעוֹת עוֹמֶס (נ"ר)
to park (vi)	laχanot	לַחֲנוֹת
to park (vt)	lehaχnot	לְהַחנוֹת
parking lot	χanaya	חֲנָיָה (נ)
subway	ra'kevet taχtit	רַכֶּבֶת תַחתִית (נ)
station	taχana	תַחֲנָה (נ)

41

to take the subway	lin'so'a betaχtit	לִנְסוֹעַ בְּתַחְתִּית
train	ra'kevet	רַכֶּבֶת (נ)
train station	taχanat ra'kevet	תַּחֲנַת רַכֶּבֶת (נ)

28. City. Life in the city

city, town	ir	עִיר (נ)
capital city	ir bira	עִיר בִּירָה (נ)
village	kfar	כְּפָר (ז)
city map	mapat ha'ir	מַפַּת הָעִיר (נ)
downtown	merkaz ha'ir	מֶרְכַּז הָעִיר (ז)
suburb	parvar	פַּרְוָר (ז)
suburban (adj)	parvari	פַּרְוָרִי
outskirts	parvar	פַּרְוָר (ז)
environs (suburbs)	svivot	סְבִיבוֹת (נ"ר)
city block	ʃχuna	שְׁכוּנָה (נ)
residential block (area)	ʃχunat megurim	שְׁכוּנַת מְגוּרִים (נ)
traffic	tnu'a	תְּנוּעָה (נ)
traffic lights	ramzor	רַמְזוֹר (ז)
public transportation	taχbura tsiburit	תַּחְבּוּרָה צִיבּוּרִית (נ)
intersection	'tsomet	צוֹמֶת (ז)
crosswalk	ma'avar χatsaya	מַעֲבָר חֲצָיָה (ז)
pedestrian underpass	ma'avar tat karka'i	מַעֲבָר תַּת־קַרְקָעִי (ז)
to cross (~ the street)	laχatsot	לַחֲצוֹת
pedestrian	holeχ 'regel	הוֹלֵךְ רֶגֶל (ז)
sidewalk	midraχa	מִדְרָכָה (נ)
bridge	'geʃer	גֶּשֶׁר (ז)
embankment (river walk)	ta'yelet	טַיֶּלֶת (נ)
fountain	mizraka	מִזְרָקָה (נ)
allée (garden walkway)	sdera	שְׂדֵרָה (נ)
park	park	פָּארק (ז)
boulevard	sdera	שְׂדֵרָה (נ)
square	kikar	כִּיכָּר (נ)
avenue (wide street)	reχov raʃi	רְחוֹב רָאשִׁי (ז)
street	reχov	רְחוֹב (ז)
side street	simta	סִמְטָה (נ)
dead end	mavoi satum	מָבוֹי סָתוּם (ז)
house	'bayit	בַּיִת (ז)
building	binyan	בִּנְיָין (ז)
skyscraper	gored ʃχakim	גּוֹרֵד שְׁחָקִים (ז)
facade	χazit	חָזִית (נ)
roof	gag	גַּג (ז)

window	χalon	חַלּוֹן (ז)
arch	'keʃet	קֶשֶׁת (נ)
column	amud	עַמּוּד (ז)
corner	pina	פִּינָה (נ)

store window	χalon ra'ava	חַלּוֹן רַאֲוָה (ז)
signboard (store sign, etc.)	'ʃelet	שֶׁלֶט (ז)
poster	kraza	כְּרָזָה (נ)
advertising poster	'poster	פּוֹסְטֶר (ז)
billboard	'luaχ pirsum	לוּחַ פִּרְסוּם (ז)

garbage, trash	'zevel	זֶבֶל (ז)
trashcan (public ~)	paχ aʃpa	פַּח אַשְׁפָּה (ז)
to litter (vi)	lelaχleχ	לְלַכְלֵךְ
garbage dump	mizbala	מִזְבָּלָה (נ)

phone booth	ta 'telefon	תָּא טֶלֶפוֹן (ז)
lamppost	amud panas	עַמּוּד פָּנָס (ז)
bench (park ~)	safsal	סַפְסָל (ז)

police officer	ʃoter	שׁוֹטֵר (ז)
police	miʃtara	מִשְׁטָרָה (נ)
beggar	kabtsan	קַבְּצָן (ז)
homeless (n)	χasar 'bayit	חֲסַר בַּיִת (ז)

29. Urban institutions

store	χanut	חֲנוּת (נ)
drugstore, pharmacy	beit mir'kaχat	בֵּית מִרְקַחַת (ז)
eyeglass store	χanut miʃka'fayim	חֲנוּת מִשְׁקָפַיִים (נ)
shopping mall	kanyon	קַנְיוֹן (ז)
supermarket	super'market	סוּפֶּרְמַרְקֶט (ז)

bakery	ma'afiya	מַאֲפִיָּה (נ)
baker	ofe	אוֹפֶה (ז)
pastry shop	χanut mamtakim	חֲנוּת מַמְתַּקִּים (נ)
grocery store	ma'kolet	מַכּוֹלֶת (נ)
butcher shop	itliz	אָטְלִיז (ז)

produce store	χanut perot viyerakot	חֲנוּת פֵּירוֹת וְיָרָקוֹת (נ)
market	ʃuk	שׁוּק (ז)

coffee house	beit kafe	בֵּית קָפֶה (ז)
restaurant	mis'ada	מִסְעָדָה (נ)
pub, bar	pab	פָּאבּ (ז)
pizzeria	pi'tseriya	פִּיצֶרְיָה (נ)

hair salon	mispara	מִסְפָּרָה (נ)
post office	'do'ar	דּוֹאַר (ז)
dry cleaners	nikui yaveʃ	נִיקּוּי יָבֵשׁ (ז)

photo studio	'studyo letsilum	סְטוּדְיוֹ לְצִילוּם (ז)
shoe store	χanut na'a'layim	חֲנוּת נַעֲלַיִים (נ)
bookstore	χanut sfarim	חֲנוּת סְפָרִים (נ)
sporting goods store	χanut sport	חֲנוּת סְפּוֹרְט (נ)
clothes repair shop	χanut tikun bgadim	חֲנוּת תִּיקוּן בְּגָדִים (נ)
formal wear rental	χanut haskarat bgadim	חֲנוּת הַשְׂכָּרַת בְּגָדִים (נ)
video rental store	χanut haʃalat sratim	חֲנוּת הַשְׁאָלַת סְרָטִים (נ)
circus	kirkas	קִרְקָס (ז)
zoo	gan hayot	גַּן חַיּוֹת (ז)
movie theater	kol'no'a	קוֹלְנוֹעַ (ז)
museum	muze'on	מוּזֵיאוֹן (ז)
library	sifriya	סִפְרִייָה (נ)
theater	te'atron	תֵּיאַטְרוֹן (ז)
opera (opera house)	beit 'opera	בֵּית אוֹפֶּרָה (ז)
nightclub	mo'adon 'laila	מוֹעֲדוֹן לַיְלָה (ז)
casino	ka'zino	קָזִינוֹ (ז)
mosque	misgad	מִסְגָּד (ז)
synagogue	beit 'kneset	בֵּית כְּנֶסֶת (ז)
cathedral	kated'rala	קָתֶדְרָלָה (נ)
temple	mikdaʃ	מִקְדָּשׁ (ז)
church	knesiya	כְּנֵסִייָה (נ)
college	miχlala	מִכְלָלָה (נ)
university	uni'versita	אוּנִיבֶרְסִיטָה (נ)
school	beit 'sefer	בֵּית סֵפֶר (ז)
prefecture	maχoz	מָחוֹז (ז)
city hall	iriya	עִירִייָה (נ)
hotel	beit malon	בֵּית מָלוֹן (ז)
bank	bank	בַּנְק (ז)
embassy	ʃagrirut	שַׁגְרִירוּת (נ)
travel agency	soχnut nesi'ot	סוֹכְנוּת נְסִיעוֹת (נ)
information office	modi'in	מוֹדִיעִין (ז)
currency exchange	misrad hamarat mat'be'a	מִשְׂרַד הֲמָרַת מַטְבֵּעַ (ז)
subway	ra'kevet taχtit	רַכֶּבֶת תַחְתִּית (נ)
hospital	beit χolim	בֵּית חוֹלִים (ז)
gas station	taχanat 'delek	תַּחֲנַת דֶלֶק (נ)
parking lot	migraʃ χanaya	מִגְרַשׁ חֲנָיָה (ז)

30. Signs

signboard (store sign, etc.)	'ʃelet	שֶׁלֶט (ז)
notice (door sign, etc.)	moda'a	מוֹדָעָה (נ)

poster	'poster	פּוֹסְטֶר (ז)
direction sign	tamrur	תַמְרוּר (ז)
arrow (sign)	χets	חֵץ (ז)
caution	azhara	אַזְהָרָה (נ)
warning sign	ʃelet azhara	שֶׁלֶט אַזְהָרָה (ז)
to warn (vt)	lehazhir	לְהַזְהִיר
rest day (weekly ~)	yom 'χofeʃ	יוֹם חוֹפֶשׁ (ז)
timetable (schedule)	'luaχ zmanim	לוּחַ זְמַנִים (ז)
opening hours	ʃa'ot avoda	שְׁעוֹת עֲבוֹדָה (נ"ר)
WELCOME!	bruχim haba'im!	בְּרוּכִים הַבָּאִים!
ENTRANCE	knisa	כְּנִיסָה
EXIT	yetsi'a	יְצִיאָה
PUSH	dχof	דְחוֹף
PULL	mʃoχ	מְשׁוֹך
OPEN	pa'tuaχ	פָּתוּחַ
CLOSED	sagur	סָגוּר
WOMEN	lenaʃim	לְנָשִׁים
MEN	legvarim	לִגְבָרִים
DISCOUNTS	hanaχot	הַנָחוֹת
SALE	mivtsa	מִבְצָע
NEW!	χadaʃ!	חָדָשׁ!
FREE	χinam	חִינָם
ATTENTION!	sim lev!	שִׂים לֵב!
NO VACANCIES	ein makom panui	אֵין מָקוֹם פָּנוּי
RESERVED	ʃamur	שָׁמוּר
ADMINISTRATION	hanhala	הַנהָלָה
STAFF ONLY	le'ovdim bilvad	לְעוֹבדִים בִּלבַד
BEWARE OF THE DOG!	zehirut 'kelev noʃeχ!	זְהִירוּת, כֶּלֶב נוֹשֵׁך!
NO SMOKING	asur le'aʃen!	אָסוּר לְעַשֵׁן!
DO NOT TOUCH!	lo lagaat!	לֹא לָגַעַת!
DANGEROUS	mesukan	מְסוּכָּן
DANGER	sakana	סַכָּנָה
HIGH VOLTAGE	'metaχ ga'voha	מֶתַח גָבוֹהַ
NO SWIMMING!	haraχatsa asura!	הָרַחָצָה אָסוּרָה!
OUT OF ORDER	lo oved	לֹא עוֹבֵד
FLAMMABLE	dalik	דָלִיק
FORBIDDEN	asur	אָסוּר
NO TRESPASSING!	asur la'avor	אָסוּר לַעֲבוֹר
WET PAINT	'tseva laχ	צֶבַע לַח

31. Shopping

to buy (purchase)	liknot	לִקְנוֹת
purchase	kniya	קְנִיָה (נ)
to go shopping	la'leχet lekniyot	לָלֶכֶת לִקְנִיוֹת
shopping	ariχat kniyot	עֲרִיכַת קְנִיוֹת (נ)
to be open (ab. store)	pa'tuaχ	פָּתוּחַ
to be closed	sagur	סָגוּר
footwear, shoes	na'a'layim	נַעֲלַיִים (נ״ר)
clothes, clothing	bgadim	בְּגָדִים (ז״ר)
cosmetics	tamrukim	תַמְרוּקִים (ז״ר)
food products	mutsrei mazon	מוּצְרֵי מָזוֹן (ז״ר)
gift, present	matana	מַתָנָה (נ)
salesman	moχer	מוֹכֵר (ז)
saleswoman	mo'χeret	מוֹכֶרֶת (נ)
check out, cash desk	kupa	קוּפָּה (נ)
mirror	mar'a	מַרְאָה (נ)
counter (store ~)	duχan	דוּכָן (ז)
fitting room	'χeder halbaʃa	חֲדָר הַלְבָּשָׁה (ז)
to try on	limdod	לִמְדוֹד
to fit (ab. dress, etc.)	lehat'im	לְהַתְאִים
to like (I like ...)	limtso χen be'ei'nayim	לִמְצוֹא חֵן בְּעֵינַיִים
price	meχir	מְחִיר (ז)
price tag	tag meχir	תַג מְחִיר (ז)
to cost (vt)	la'alot	לַעֲלוֹת
How much?	'kama?	כַּמָה?
discount	hanaχa	הֲנָחָה (נ)
inexpensive (adj)	lo yakar	לֹא יָקָר
cheap (adj)	zol	זוֹל
expensive (adj)	yakar	יָקָר
It's expensive	ze yakar	זֶה יָקָר
rental (n)	haskara	הַשְׂכָּרָה (נ)
to rent (~ a tuxedo)	liskor	לִשְׂכּוֹר
credit (trade credit)	aʃrai	אַשְׁרַאי (ז)
on credit (adv)	be'aʃrai	בְּאַשְׁרַאי

CLOTHING & ACCESSORIES

32. Outerwear. Coats

clothes	bgadim	בְּגָדִים (ז"ר)
outerwear	levuʃ elyon	לְבוּשׁ עֶלְיוֹן (ז)
winter clothing	bigdei 'χoref	בִּגְדֵי חוֹרֶף (ז"ר)
coat (overcoat)	me'il	מְעִיל (ז)
fur coat	me'il parva	מְעִיל פַּרְוָה (ז)
fur jacket	me'il parva katsar	מְעִיל פַּרְוָה קָצָר (ז)
down coat	me'il puχ	מְעִיל פּוּךְ (ז)
jacket (e.g., leather ~)	me'il katsar	מְעִיל קָצָר (ז)
raincoat (trenchcoat, etc.)	me'il 'geʃem	מְעִיל גֶּשֶׁם (ז)
waterproof (adj)	amid be'mayim	עָמִיד בְּמַיִם

33. Men's & women's clothing

shirt (button shirt)	χultsa	חוּלְצָה (נ)
pants	miχna'sayim	מִכְנָסַיִים (ז"ר)
jeans	miχnesei 'dʒins	מִכְנְסֵי גִ'ינְס (ז"ר)
suit jacket	ʒaket	זָ'קֶט (ז)
suit	χalifa	חֲלִיפָה (נ)
dress (frock)	simla	שִׂמְלָה (נ)
skirt	χatsa'it	חֲצָאִית (נ)
blouse	χultsa	חוּלְצָה (נ)
knitted jacket (cardigan, etc.)	ʒaket 'tsemer	זָ'קֶט צֶמֶר (ז)
jacket (of woman's suit)	ʒaket	זָ'קֶט (ז)
T-shirt	ti ʃert	טִי שֶׁרְט (ז)
shorts (short trousers)	miχna'sayim ktsarim	מִכְנָסַיִים קְצָרִים (ז"ר)
tracksuit	'trening	טְרֶנִינְג (ז)
bathrobe	χaluk raχatsa	חָלוּק רַחְצָה (ז)
pajamas	pi'dʒama	פִּיגָ'מָה (נ)
sweater	'sveder	סְוֶוד̇ר (ז)
pullover	afuda	אֲפוּדָה (נ)
vest	vest	וֶסְט (ז)
tailcoat	frak	פְרָאק (ז)
tuxedo	tuk'sido	טוּקְסִידוֹ (ז)

uniform	madim	מַדִים (ז"ר)
workwear	bigdei avoda	בִּגְדֵי עֲבוֹדָה (ז"ר)
overalls	sarbal	סַרְבָּל (ז)
coat (e.g., doctor's smock)	xaluk	חָלוּק (ז)

34. Clothing. Underwear

underwear	levanim	לְבָנִים (ז"ר)
boxers, briefs	taxtonim	תַחְתוֹנִים (ז"ר)
panties	taxtonim	תַחְתוֹנִים (ז"ר)
undershirt (A-shirt)	gufiya	גוּפִיָּה (נ)
socks	gar'bayim	גַרְבַּיִם (ז"ר)
nightgown	'ktonet 'laila	כְּתוֹנֶת לַיְלָה (נ)
bra	xaziya	חֲזִיָּה (נ)
knee highs (knee-high socks)	birkon	בִּרְכּוֹן (ז)
pantyhose	garbonim	גַרְבּוֹנִים (ז"ר)
stockings (thigh highs)	garbei 'nailon	גַרְבֵּי נַיְלוֹן (ז"ר)
bathing suit	'beged yam	בֶּגֶד יָם (ז)

35. Headwear

hat	'kova	כּוֹבַע (ז)
fedora	'kova 'leved	כּוֹבַע לֶבֶד (ז)
baseball cap	'kova 'beisbol	כּוֹבַע בֵּייסְבּוֹל (ז)
flatcap	'kova mitsxiya	כּוֹבַע מִצְחִיָּה (ז)
beret	baret	בֶּרֶט (ז)
hood	bardas	בַּרְדָס (ז)
panama hat	'kova 'tembel	כּוֹבַע טֶמְבֶּל (ז)
knit cap (knitted hat)	'kova 'gerev	כּוֹבַע גֶרֶב (ז)
headscarf	mit'paxat	מִטְפַּחַת (נ)
women's hat	'kova	כּוֹבַע (ז)
hard hat	kasda	קַסְדָה (נ)
garrison cap	kumta	כּוּמְתָה (נ)
helmet	kasda	קַסְדָה (נ)
derby	mig'ba'at me'u'gelet	מִגְבַּעַת מְעוּגֶלֶת (נ)
top hat	tsi'linder	צִילִינְדֶר (ז)

36. Footwear

footwear	han'ala	הַנְעָלָה (נ)
shoes (men's shoes)	na'a'layim	נַעֲלַיִם (נ"ר)

shoes (women's shoes)	na'a'layim	נַעֲלַיִם (נ"ר)
boots (e.g., cowboy ~)	maga'fayim	מַגָּפַיִם (נ"ר)
slippers	na'alei 'bayit	נַעֲלֵי בַּיִת (נ"ר)
tennis shoes (e.g., Nike ~)	na'alei sport	נַעֲלֵי ספּוֹרט (נ"ר)
sneakers (e.g., Converse ~)	na'alei sport	נַעֲלֵי ספּוֹרט (נ"ר)
sandals	sandalim	סַנדָּלִים (ז"ר)
cobbler (shoe repairer)	sandlar	סַנדּלָר (ז)
heel	akev	עָקֵב (ז)
pair (of shoes)	zug	זוּג (ז)
shoestring	sroχ	שׂרוֹךְ (ז)
to lace (vt)	lisroχ	לִשׂרוֹךְ
shoehorn	kaf na'a'layim	כַּף נַעֲלַיִם (נ)
shoe polish	miʃχat na'a'layim	מִשחַת נַעֲלַיִם (נ)

37. Personal accessories

gloves	kfafot	כּפָפוֹת (נ"ר)
mittens	kfafot	כּפָפוֹת (נ"ר)
scarf (muffler)	tsa'if	צָעִיף (ז)
glasses (eyeglasses)	miʃka'fayim	מִשקָפַיִם (ז"ר)
frame (eyeglass ~)	mis'geret	מִסגֶרֶת (נ)
umbrella	mitriya	מִטרִיָה (נ)
walking stick	makel haliχa	מַקֵל הֲלִיכָה (ז)
hairbrush	miv'reʃet se'ar	מִברֶשֶת שֵׂיעָר (נ)
fan	menifa	מְנִיפָה (נ)
tie (necktie)	aniva	עֲנִיבָה (נ)
bow tie	anivat parpar	עֲנִיבַת פַּרפַּר (נ)
suspenders	ktefiyot	כּתֵפִיוֹת (נ"ר)
handkerchief	mimχata	מִמחָטָה (נ)
comb	masrek	מַסרֵק (ז)
barrette	sikat roʃ	סִיכַּת רֹאש (נ)
hairpin	sikat se'ar	סִיכַּת שֵׂעָר (נ)
buckle	avzam	אַבזָם (ז)
belt	χagora	חֲגוֹרָה (נ)
shoulder strap	retsu'at katef	רְצוּעַת כָּתֵף (נ)
bag (handbag)	tik	תִיק (ז)
purse	tik	תִיק (ז)
backpack	tarmil	תַרמִיל (ז)

38. Clothing. Miscellaneous

fashion	ofna	אוֹפְנָה (נ)
in vogue (adj)	ofnati	אוֹפְנָתִי
fashion designer	me'atsev ofna	מְעַצֵב אוֹפְנָה (ז)
collar	tsavaron	צַוָארוֹן (ז)
pocket	kis	כִּיס (ז)
pocket (as adj)	ʃel kis	שֶל כִּיס
sleeve	ʃarvul	שַרווּל (ז)
hanging loop	mitle	מִתלֶה (ז)
fly (on trousers)	χanut	חֲנוּת (נ)
zipper (fastener)	roχsan	רוֹכסָן (ז)
fastener	'keres	קֶרֶס (ז)
button	kaftor	כַּפתוֹר (ז)
buttonhole	lula'a	לוּלָאָה (נ)
to come off (ab. button)	lehitaleʃ	לְהִיתָלֵש
to sew (vi, vt)	litpor	לִתפוֹר
to embroider (vi, vt)	lirkom	לִרקוֹם
embroidery	rikma	רִקמָה (נ)
sewing needle	'maχat tfira	מַחַט תפִירָה (נ)
thread	χut	חוּט (ז)
seam	'tefer	תֶפֶר (ז)
to get dirty (vi)	lehitlaχleχ	לְהִתלַכלֵך
stain (mark, spot)	'ketem	כֶּתֶם (ז)
to crease, crumple (vi)	lehitkamet	לְהִתקַמֵט
to tear, to rip (vt)	lik'ro'a	לִקרוֹעַ
clothes moth	aʃ	עָש (ז)

39. Personal care. Cosmetics

toothpaste	miʃχat ʃi'nayim	מִשחַת שִינַיִים (נ)
toothbrush	miv'reʃet ʃi'nayim	מִברֶשֶת שִינַיִים (נ)
to brush one's teeth	letsaχ'tseaχ ʃi'nayim	לְצַחצֵחַ שִינַיִים
razor	'ta'ar	תַעַר (ז)
shaving cream	'ketsef gi'luaχ	קֶצֶף גִילוּחַ (ז)
to shave (vi)	lehitga'leaχ	לְהִתגַלֵחַ
soap	sabon	סַבּוֹן (ז)
shampoo	ʃampu	שַמפּוּ (ז)
scissors	mispa'rayim	מִספָּרַיִים (ז"ר)
nail file	ptsira	פצִירָה (נ)
nail clippers	gozez tsipor'nayim	גוֹזֵז צִיפּוֹרנַיִים (ז)
tweezers	pin'tseta	פִינצֶטָה (נ)

cosmetics	tamrukim	תַּמְרוּקִים (ז"ר)
face mask	masexa	מַסֵכָה (נ)
manicure	manikur	מָנִיקוּר (ז)
to have a manicure	la'asot manikur	לַעֲשׂוֹת מָנִיקוּר
pedicure	pedikur	פֶּדִיקוּר (ז)
make-up bag	tik ipur	תִּיק אִיפּוּר (ז)
face powder	'pudra	פּוּדְרָה (נ)
powder compact	pudriya	פּוּדְרִיָּה (נ)
blusher	'somek	סוֹמֶק (ז)
perfume (bottled)	'bosem	בּוֹשֶׂם (ז)
toilet water (lotion)	mei 'bosem	מֵי בּוֹשֶׂם (ז"ר)
lotion	mei panim	מֵי פָּנִים (ז"ר)
cologne	mei 'bosem	מֵי בּוֹשֶׂם (ז"ר)
eyeshadow	tslalit	צְלָלִית (נ)
eyeliner	ai 'lainer	אַי לַיְינֶר (ז)
mascara	'maskara	מַסְקָרָה (נ)
lipstick	sfaton	שְׂפָתוֹן (ז)
nail polish, enamel	'laka letsipor'nayim	לַכָּה לְצִיפּוֹרְנַיִם (נ)
hair spray	tarsis lese'ar	תַּרְסִיס לְשֵׂיעָר (ז)
deodorant	de'odo'rant	דָּאוֹדוֹרַנט (ז)
cream	krem	קְרֶם (ז)
face cream	krem panim	קְרֶם פָּנִים (ז)
hand cream	krem ya'dayim	קְרֶם יָדַיִים (ז)
anti-wrinkle cream	krem 'neged kmatim	קְרֶם נֶגֶד קְמָטִים (ז)
day cream	krem yom	קְרֶם יוֹם (ז)
night cream	krem 'laila	קְרֶם לַיְלָה (ז)
day (as adj)	yomi	יוֹמִי
night (as adj)	leili	לֵילִי
tampon	tampon	טַמְפּוֹן (ז)
toilet paper (toilet roll)	neyar tu'alet	נְיָיר טוּאָלֶט (ז)
hair dryer	meyabef se'ar	מְיַיבֵּשׁ שֵׂיעָר (ז)

40. Watches. Clocks

watch (wristwatch)	fe'on yad	שְׁעוֹן יָד (ז)
dial	'luax fa'on	לוּחַ שָׁעוֹן (ז)
hand (of clock, watch)	maxog	מָחוֹג (ז)
metal watch band	tsamid	צָמִיד (ז)
watch strap	retsu'a lefa'on	רְצוּעָה לְשָׁעוֹן (נ)
battery	solela	סוֹלְלָה (נ)
to be dead (battery)	lehitroken	לְהִתְרוֹקֵן
to change a battery	lehaxlif	לְהַחְלִיף
to run fast	lemaher	לְמַהֵר

to run slow	lefager	לְפַגֵּר
wall clock	ʃeʾon kir	שְׁעוֹן קִיר (ז)
hourglass	ʃeʾon χol	שְׁעוֹן חוֹל (ז)
sundial	ʃeʾon 'ʃemeʃ	שְׁעוֹן שֶׁמֶשׁ (ז)
alarm clock	ʃaʾon meʾorer	שְׁעוֹן מְעוֹרֵר (ז)
watchmaker	ʃaʾan	שָׁעָן (ז)
to repair (vt)	letaken	לְתַקֵּן

EVERYDAY EXPERIENCE

41. Money

money	'kesef	כֶּסֶף (ז)
currency exchange	hamara	הֲמָרָה (נ)
exchange rate	'ʃa'ar χalifin	שַׁעַר חֲלִיפִין (ז)
ATM	kaspomat	כַּספּוֹמָט (ז)
coin	mat'be'a	מַטבֵּעַ (ז)
dollar	'dolar	דּוֹלָר (ז)
euro	'eiro	אֵירוֹ (ז)
lira	'lira	לִירָה (נ)
Deutschmark	mark germani	מַרק גֶּרמָנִי (ז)
franc	frank	פּרַנק (ז)
pound sterling	'lira 'sterling	לִירָה שטֶרלִינג (נ)
yen	yen	יֶן (ז)
debt	χov	חוֹב (ז)
debtor	'ba'al χov	בַּעַל חוֹב (ז)
to lend (money)	lehalvot	לְהַלווֹת
to borrow (vi, vt)	lilvot	לִלווֹת
bank	bank	בַּנק (ז)
account	χeʃbon	חֶשבּוֹן (ז)
to deposit (vt)	lehafkid	לְהַפקִיד
to deposit into the account	lehafkid leχeʃbon	לְהַפקִיד לְחֶשבּוֹן
to withdraw (vt)	limʃoχ meχeʃbon	לִמשוֹך מֵחֶשבּוֹן
credit card	kartis aʃrai	כַּרטִיס אַשרַאי (ז)
cash	mezuman	מְזוּמָן
check	tʃek	צֶ'ק (ז)
to write a check	liχtov tʃek	לִכתוֹב צֶ'ק
checkbook	pinkas 'tʃekim	פִּנקָס צֶ'קִים (ז)
wallet	arnak	אַרנָק (ז)
change purse	arnak lematbe''ot	אַרנָק לְמַטבְּעוֹת (ז)
safe	ka'sefet	כַּסֶפֶת (נ)
heir	yoreʃ	יוֹרֵש (ז)
inheritance	yeruʃa	יְרוּשָה (נ)
fortune (wealth)	'oʃer	עוֹשֶר (ז)
lease	χoze sχirut	חוֹזֶה שכִירוּת (ז)
rent (money)	sχar dira	שכַר דִּירָה (ז)

to rent (sth from sb)	liskor	לִשְׂכּוֹר
price	meχir	מְחִיר (ז)
cost	alut	עֲלוּת (נ)
sum	sχum	סְכוּם (ז)
to spend (vt)	lehotsi	לְהוֹצִיא
expenses	hotsa'ot	הוֹצָאוֹת (נ"ר)
to economize (vi, vt)	laχasoχ	לַחֲסוֹךְ
economical	χesχoni	חֶסְכוֹנִי
to pay (vi, vt)	leʃalem	לְשַׁלֵם
payment	taʃlum	תַּשְׁלוּם (ז)
change (give the ~)	'odef	עוֹדֶף (ז)
tax	mas	מַס (ז)
fine	knas	קְנָס (ז)
to fine (vt)	liknos	לִקְנוֹס

42. Post. Postal service

post office	'do'ar	דּוֹאַר (ז)
mail (letters, etc.)	'do'ar	דּוֹאַר (ז)
mailman	davar	דַּוָּר (ז)
opening hours	ʃa'ot avoda	שְׁעוֹת עֲבוֹדָה (נ"ר)
letter	miχtav	מִכְתָּב (ז)
registered letter	miχtav raʃum	מִכְתָּב רָשׁוּם (ז)
postcard	gluya	גְּלוּיָה (נ)
telegram	mivrak	מִבְרָק (ז)
package (parcel)	χavila	חֲבִילָה (נ)
money transfer	ha'avarat ksafim	הַעֲבָרַת כְּסָפִים (נ)
to receive (vt)	lekabel	לְקַבֵּל
to send (vt)	liʃ'loaχ	לִשְׁלוֹחַ
sending	ʃliχa	שְׁלִיחָה (נ)
address	'ktovet	כְּתוֹבֶת (נ)
ZIP code	mikud	מִיקּוּד (ז)
sender	ʃo'leaχ	שׁוֹלֵחַ (ז)
receiver	nim'an	נִמְעָן (ז)
name (first name)	ʃem prati	שֵׁם פְּרָטִי (ז)
surname (last name)	ʃem miʃpaχa	שֵׁם מִשְׁפָּחָה (ז)
postage rate	ta'arif	תַּעֲרִיף (ז)
standard (adj)	ragil	רָגִיל
economical (adj)	χesχoni	חֶסְכוֹנִי
weight	miʃkal	מִשְׁקָל (ז)
to weigh (~ letters)	liʃkol	לִשְׁקוֹל

envelope	ma'atafa	מַעֲטָפָה (נ)
postage stamp	bul 'do'ar	בּוּל דּוֹאַר (ז)
to stamp an envelope	lehadbik bul	לְהַדְבִּיק בּוּל

43. Banking

bank	bank	בַּנק (ז)
branch (of bank, etc.)	snif	סְנִיף (ז)
bank clerk, consultant	yo'ets	יוֹעֵץ (ז)
manager (director)	menahel	מְנַהֵל (ז)
bank account	xeʃbon	חֶשׁבּוֹן (ז)
account number	mispar xeʃbon	מִספַּר חֶשׁבּוֹן (ז)
checking account	xeʃbon over vaʃav	חֶשׁבּוֹן עוֹבֵר וָשָׁב (ז)
savings account	xeʃbon xisaxon	חֶשׁבּוֹן חִסָכוֹן (ז)
to open an account	lif'toax xeʃbon	לִפתוֹחַ חֶשׁבּוֹן
to close the account	lisgor xeʃbon	לִסגוֹר חֶשׁבּוֹן
to deposit into the account	lehafkid lexeʃbon	לְהַפקִיד לַחֶשׁבּוֹן
to withdraw (vt)	limʃox mexeʃbon	לִמשׁוֹך מֵחֶשׁבּוֹן
deposit	pikadon	פִּיקָדוֹן (ז)
to make a deposit	lehafkid	לְהַפקִיד
wire transfer	ha'avara banka'it	הַעֲבָרָה בַּנקָאִית (נ)
to wire, to transfer	leha'avir 'kesef	לְהַעֲבִיר כֶּסֶף
sum	sxum	סכוּם (ז)
How much?	'kama?	כַּמָה?
signature	xatima	חֲתִימָה (נ)
to sign (vt)	laxtom	לַחתוֹם
credit card	kartis aʃrai	כַּרטִיס אַשׁרַאי (ז)
code (PIN code)	kod	קוֹד (ז)
credit card number	mispar kartis aʃrai	מִספַּר כַּרטִיס אַשׁרַאי (ז)
ATM	kaspomat	כַּספּוֹמָט (ז)
check	tʃek	צֶ'ק (ז)
to write a check	lixtov tʃek	לִכתוֹב צֶ'ק
checkbook	pinkas 'tʃekim	פִּנקָס צֶ'קִים (ז)
loan (bank ~)	halva'a	הַלוָואָה (נ)
to apply for a loan	levakeʃ halva'a	לְבַקֵשׁ הַלוָואָה
to get a loan	lekabel halva'a	לְקַבֵּל הַלוָואָה
to give a loan	lehalvot	לְהַלווֹת
guarantee	arvut	עַרבוּת (נ)

44. Telephone. Phone conversation

telephone	'telefon	טֶלֶפוֹן (ז)
cell phone	'telefon nayad	טֶלֶפוֹן נַיָּיד (ז)
answering machine	meʃivon	מְשִׁיבוֹן (ז)

| to call (by phone) | letsaltsel | לְצַלְצֵל |
| phone call | siχat 'telefon | שִׂיחַת טֶלֶפוֹן (נ) |

to dial a number	leχayeg mispar	לְחַיֵּיג מִסְפָּר
Hello!	'halo!	הַלוֹ!
to ask (vt)	liʃol	לִשְׁאוֹל
to answer (vi, vt)	la'anot	לַעֲנוֹת

to hear (vt)	liʃmo'a	לִשְׁמוֹעַ
well (adv)	tov	טוֹב
not well (adv)	lo tov	לֹא טוֹב
noises (interference)	hafra'ot	הַפְרָעוֹת (נ"ר)

receiver	ʃfo'feret	שְׁפוֹפֶרֶת (נ)
to pick up (~ the phone)	leharim ʃfo'feret	לְהָרִים שְׁפוֹפֶרֶת
to hang up (~ the phone)	leha'niaχ ʃfo'feret	לְהַנִּיחַ שְׁפוֹפֶרֶת

busy (engaged)	tafus	תָּפוּס
to ring (ab. phone)	letsaltsel	לְצַלְצֵל
telephone book	'sefer tele'fonim	סֵפֶר טֶלֶפוֹנִים (ז)

local (adj)	mekomi	מְקוֹמִי
local call	siχa mekomit	שִׂיחָה מְקוֹמִית (נ)
long distance (~ call)	bein ironi	בֵּין עִירוֹנִי
long-distance call	siχa bein ironit	שִׂיחָה בֵּין עִירוֹנִית (נ)
international (adj)	benle'umi	בֵּינְלְאוּמִי
international call	siχa benle'umit	שִׂיחָה בֵּינְלְאוּמִית (נ)

45. Cell phone

cell phone	'telefon nayad	טֶלֶפוֹן נַיָּיד (ז)
display	masaχ	מָסָךְ (ז)
button	kaftor	כַּפְתּוֹר (ז)
SIM card	kartis sim	כַּרְטִיס סִים (ז)

battery	solela	סוֹלְלָה (נ)
to be dead (battery)	lehitroken	לְהִתְרוֹקֵן
charger	mit'an	מִטְעָן (ז)

menu	tafrit	תַּפְרִיט (ז)
settings	hagdarot	הַגְדָּרוֹת (נ"ר)
tune (melody)	mangina	מַנְגִּינָה (נ)
to select (vt)	livχor	לִבְחוֹר

calculator	maxʃevon	מַחשְׁבוֹן (ז)
voice mail	ta koli	תָּא קוֹלִי (ז)
alarm clock	ʃa'on me'orer	שָׁעוֹן מְעוֹרֵר (ז)
contacts	anʃei 'keʃer	אַנשֵׁי קֶשֶׁר (ז"ר)
SMS (text message)	misron	מִסרוֹן (ז)
subscriber	manui	מָנוּי (ז)

46. Stationery

ballpoint pen	et kaduri	עֵט כַּדוּרִי (ז)
fountain pen	et no've'a	עֵט נוֹבֵעַ (ז)
pencil	iparon	עִיפָּרוֹן (ז)
highlighter	'marker	מַרקֵר (ז)
felt-tip pen	tuʃ	טוּשׁ (ז)
notepad	pinkas	פִּנקָס (ז)
agenda (diary)	yoman	יוֹמָן (ז)
ruler	sargel	סַרגֵּל (ז)
calculator	maxʃevon	מַחשְׁבוֹן (ז)
eraser	'maxak	מַחַק (ז)
thumbtack	'na'ats	נַעַץ (ז)
paper clip	mehadek	מְהַדֵק (ז)
glue	'devek	דֶבֶק (ז)
stapler	ʃadxan	שַׁדכָן (ז)
hole punch	menakev	מְנַקֵב (ז)
pencil sharpener	maxded	מַחְדֵד (ז)

47. Foreign languages

language	safa	שָׂפָה (נ)
foreign (adj)	zar	זָר
foreign language	safa zara	שָׂפָה זָרָה (נ)
to study (vt)	lilmod	לִלמוֹד
to learn (language, etc.)	lilmod	לִלמוֹד
to read (vi, vt)	likro	לִקרוֹא
to speak (vi, vt)	ledaber	לְדַבֵּר
to understand (vt)	lehavin	לְהָבִין
to write (vt)	lixtov	לִכתוֹב
fast (adv)	maher	מַהֵר
slowly (adv)	le'at	לְאַט
fluently (adv)	xofʃi	חוֹפשִׁי
rules	klalim	כְּלָלִים (ז"ר)

grammar	dikduk	דִקדוּק (ז)
vocabulary	otsar milim	אוֹצַר מִילִים (ז)
phonetics	torat ha'hege	תוֹרַת הַהֶגָה (נ)
textbook	'sefer limud	סֵפֶר לִימוּד (ז)
dictionary	milon	מִילוֹן (ז)
teach-yourself book	'sefer lelimud atsmi	סֵפֶר לְלִימוּד עַצמִי (ז)
phrasebook	siχon	שִׂיחוֹן (ז)
cassette, tape	ka'letet	קַלֶטֶת (נ)
videotape	ka'letet 'vide'o	קַלֶטֶת וִידֵיאוֹ (נ)
CD, compact disc	taklitor	תַקלִיטוֹר (ז)
DVD	di vi di	דִי. וִי. דִי. (ז)
alphabet	alefbeit	אָלֶפבֵּית (ז)
to spell (vt)	le'ayet	לְאַיֵית
pronunciation	hagiya	הֲגִייָה (נ)
accent	mivta	מִבטָא (ז)
with an accent	im mivta	עִם מִבטָא
without an accent	bli mivta	בּלִי מִבטָא
word	mila	מִילָה (נ)
meaning	maʃma'ut	מַשמָעוּת (נ)
course (e.g., a French ~)	kurs	קוּרס (ז)
to sign up	leheraʃem lekurs	לְהֵירָשֵם לְקוּרס
teacher	more	מוֹרֶה (ז)
translation (process)	tirgum	תִרגוּם (ז)
translation (text, etc.)	tirgum	תִרגוּם (ז)
translator	metargem	מְתַרגֵם (ז)
interpreter	meturgeman	מְתוּרגְמָן (ז)
polyglot	poliglot	פּוֹלִיגלוֹט (ז)
memory	zikaron	זִיכָּרוֹן (ז)

MEALS. RESTAURANT

48. Table setting

spoon	kaf	כַּף (ז)
knife	sakin	סַכִּין (ז, נ)
fork	mazleg	מַזְלֵג (ז)
cup (e.g., coffee ~)	'sefel	סֵפֶל (ז)
plate (dinner ~)	tsa'laxat	צַלַחַת (נ)
saucer	taxtit	תַחְתִּית (נ)
napkin (on table)	mapit	מַפִּית (נ)
toothpick	keisam ʃi'nayim	קֵיסָם שִׁינַיִים (ז)

49. Restaurant

restaurant	mis'ada	מִסְעָדָה (נ)
coffee house	beit kafe	בֵּית קָפֶה (ז)
pub, bar	bar, pab	בָּר, פָּאב (ז)
tearoom	beit te	בֵּית תָה (ז)
waiter	meltsar	מֶלְצָר (ז)
waitress	meltsarit	מֶלְצָרִית (נ)
bartender	'barmen	בַּרְמֶן (ז)
menu	tafrit	תַפְרִיט (ז)
wine list	reʃimat yeynot	רְשִׁימַת יֵינוֹת (נ)
to book a table	lehazmin ʃulxan	לְהַזְמִין שׁוּלְחָן
course, dish	mana	מָנָה (נ)
to order (meal)	lehazmin	לְהַזְמִין
to make an order	lehazmin	לְהַזְמִין
aperitif	maʃke meta'aven	מַשְׁקֶה מְתַאַבֵן (ז)
appetizer	meta'aven	מְתַאַבֵן (ז)
dessert	ki'nuax	קִינוּחַ (ז)
check	xeʃbon	חֶשְׁבּוֹן (ז)
to pay the check	leʃalem	לְשַׁלֵם
to give change	latet 'odef	לָתֵת עוֹדֶף
tip	tip	טִיפּ (ז)

50. Meals

food	'oxel	אוֹכֶל (ז)
to eat (vi, vt)	le'exol	לֶאֱכוֹל
breakfast	aruxat 'boker	אֲרוּחַת בּוֹקֶר (נ)
to have breakfast	le'exol aruxat 'boker	לֶאֱכוֹל אֲרוּחַת בּוֹקֶר
lunch	aruxat tsaha'rayim	אֲרוּחַת צָהֳרַיִם (נ)
to have lunch	le'exol aruxat tsaha'rayim	לֶאֱכוֹל אֲרוּחַת צָהֳרַיִם
dinner	aruxat 'erev	אֲרוּחַת עֶרֶב (נ)
to have dinner	le'exol aruxat 'erev	לֶאֱכוֹל אֲרוּחַת עֶרֶב
appetite	te'avon	תֵּיאָבוֹן (ז)
Enjoy your meal!	betei'avon!	בְּתֵיאָבוֹן!
to open (~ a bottle)	lif'toax	לִפְתוֹחַ
to spill (liquid)	liʃpox	לִשְׁפּוֹךְ
to spill out (vi)	lehiʃapex	לְהִישָׁפֵךְ
to boil (vi)	lir'toax	לִרְתוֹחַ
to boil (vt)	lehar'tiax	לְהַרְתִּיחַ
boiled (~ water)	ra'tuax	רָתוּחַ
to chill, cool down (vt)	lekarer	לְקָרֵר
to chill (vi)	lehitkarer	לְהִתְקָרֵר
taste, flavor	'ta'am	טַעַם (ז)
aftertaste	'ta'am levai	טַעַם לְוַואי (ז)
to slim down (lose weight)	lirzot	לִרְזוֹת
diet	di''eta	דִּיאֶטָה (נ)
vitamin	vitamin	וִיטָמִין (ז)
calorie	ka'lorya	קָלוֹרִיָה (נ)
vegetarian (n)	tsimxoni	צִמְחוֹנִי (ז)
vegetarian (adj)	tsimxoni	צִמְחוֹנִי
fats (nutrient)	ʃumanim	שׁוּמָנִים (ז"ר)
proteins	xelbonim	חֶלְבּוֹנִים (ז"ר)
carbohydrates	paxmema	פַּחְמֵימָה (נ)
slice (of lemon, ham)	prusa	פְּרוּסָה (נ)
piece (of cake, pie)	xatixa	חֲתִיכָה (נ)
crumb (of bread, cake, etc.)	perur	פֵּירוּר (ז)

51. Cooked dishes

course, dish	mana	מָנָה (נ)
cuisine	mitbax	מִטְבָּח (ז)
recipe	matkon	מַתְכּוֹן (ז)
portion	mana	מָנָה (נ)

salad	salat	סָלָט (ז)
soup	marak	מָרָק (ז)
clear soup (broth)	marak tsaχ, tsir	מָרָק צַח, צִיר (ז)
sandwich (bread)	kariχ	כָּרִיך (ז)
fried eggs	beitsat ain	בֵּיצַת עַיִן (נ)
hamburger (beefburger)	'hamburger	הַמבּוּרגֶר (ז)
beefsteak	umtsa, steik	אוּמצָה (נ), סטֵייק (ז)
side dish	to'sefet	תוֹסֶפֶת (נ)
spaghetti	spa'geti	סְפָּגֶטִי (ז)
mashed potatoes	meχit tapuχei adama	מְחִית תַפּוּחֵי אֲדָמָה (נ)
pizza	'pitsa	פִּיצָה (נ)
porridge (oatmeal, etc.)	daysa	דַייסָה (נ)
omelet	χavita	חֲבִיתָה (נ)
boiled (e.g., ~ beef)	mevuʃal	מְבוּשָל
smoked (adj)	me'uʃan	מְעוּשָן
fried (adj)	metugan	מְטוּגָן
dried (adj)	meyubaʃ	מְיוּבָּש
frozen (adj)	kafu	קָפוּא
pickled (adj)	kavuʃ	כָּבוּש
sweet (sugary)	matok	מָתוֹק
salty (adj)	ma'luaχ	מָלוּחַ
cold (adj)	kar	קָר
hot (adj)	χam	חַם
bitter (adj)	marir	מָרִיר
tasty (adj)	ta'im	טָעִים
to cook in boiling water	levaʃel be'mayim rotχim	לְבַשֵל בְּמַיִם רוֹתחִים
to cook (dinner)	levaʃel	לְבַשֵל
to fry (vt)	letagen	לְטַגֵן
to heat up (food)	leχamem	לְחַמֵם
to salt (vt)	leham'liaχ	לְהַמלִיחַ
to pepper (vt)	lefalpel	לְפַלפֵּל
to grate (vt)	lerasek	לְרַסֵק
peel (n)	klipa	קלִיפָּה (נ)
to peel (vt)	lekalef	לְקַלֵף

52. Food

meat	basar	בָּשָׂר (ז)
chicken	of	עוֹף (ז)
Rock Cornish hen (poussin)	pargit	פַּרגִית (נ)
duck	barvaz	בַּרווָז (ז)
goose	avaz	אַווָז (ז)

game	'tsayid	צַיִד (ז)
turkey	'hodu	הוֹדוּ (ז)
pork	basar xazir	בָּשָׂר חֲזִיר (ז)
veal	basar 'egel	בָּשָׂר עֵגֶל (ז)
lamb	basar 'keves	בָּשָׂר כֶּבֶשׂ (ז)
beef	bakar	בָּקָר (ז)
rabbit	arnav	אַרְנָב (ז)
sausage (bologna, pepperoni, etc.)	naknik	נַקְנִיק (ז)
vienna sausage (frankfurter)	naknikiya	נַקְנִיקִיָּה (נ)
bacon	'kotel xazir	קוֹתֶל חֲזִיר (ז)
ham	basar xazir me'uʃan	בָּשָׂר חֲזִיר מְעוּשָׁן (ז)
gammon	'kotel xazir me'uʃan	קוֹתֶל חֲזִיר מְעוּשָׁן (ז)
pâté	pate	פָּטֶה (ז)
liver	kaved	כָּבֵד (ז)
hamburger (ground beef)	basar taxun	בָּשָׂר טָחוּן (ז)
tongue	laʃon	לָשׁוֹן (נ)
egg	beitsa	בֵּיצָה (נ)
eggs	beitsim	בֵּיצִים (נ"ר)
egg white	xelbon	חֶלְבּוֹן (ז)
egg yolk	xelmon	חֶלְמוֹן (ז)
fish	dag	דָּג (ז)
seafood	perot yam	פֵּירוֹת יָם (ז"ר)
crustaceans	sartana'im	סַרְטָנָאִים (ז"ר)
caviar	kavyar	קָוְויָאר (ז)
crab	sartan yam	סַרְטָן יָם (ז)
shrimp	ʃrimps	שְׁרִימְפְּס (ז"ר)
oyster	tsidpat ma'axal	צִדְפַּת מַאֲכָל (נ)
spiny lobster	'lobster kotsani	לוֹבְּסְטֶר קוֹצָנִי (ז)
octopus	tamnun	תַּמְנוּן (ז)
squid	kala'mari	קָלָמָארִי (ז)
sturgeon	basar haxidkan	בָּשָׂר הַחִדְקָן (ז)
salmon	'salmon	סַלְמוֹן (ז)
halibut	putit	פּוּטִית (נ)
cod	ʃibut	שִׁיבּוּט (ז)
mackerel	kolyas	קוֹלְיָס (ז)
tuna	'tuna	טוּנָה (נ)
eel	tslofax	צְלוֹפָח (ז)
trout	forel	פוֹרֶל (ז)
sardine	sardin	סַרְדִּין (ז)
pike	ze'ev 'mayim	זְאֵב מַיִם (ז)
herring	ma'liax	מָלִיחַ (ז)

bread	'leχem	לֶחֶם (ז)
cheese	gvina	גְבִינָה (נ)
sugar	sukar	סוֹכָּר (ז)
salt	'melaχ	מֶלַח (ז)
rice	'orez	אוֹרֶז (ז)
pasta (macaroni)	'pasta	פַּסטָה (נ)
noodles	irtiyot	אָטרִיוֹת (נ"ר)
butter	χem'a	חֶמאָה (נ)
vegetable oil	'ʃemen tsimχi	שֶמֶן צָמחִי (ז)
sunflower oil	'ʃemen χamaniyot	שֶמֶן חַמָנִיוֹת (ז)
margarine	marga'rina	מַרגָרִינָה (נ)
olives	zeitim	זֵיתִים (ז"ר)
olive oil	'ʃemen 'zayit	שֶמֶן זַיִת (ז)
milk	χalav	חָלָב (ז)
condensed milk	χalav merukaz	חָלָב מְרוּכָּז (ז)
yogurt	'yogurt	יוֹגוּרט (ז)
sour cream	ʃa'menet	שַמֶנֶת (נ)
cream (of milk)	ʃa'menet	שַמֶנֶת (נ)
mayonnaise	mayonez	מָיוֹנֶז (ז)
buttercream	ka'tsefet χem'a	קַצֶפֶת חָמאָה (נ)
cereal grains (wheat, etc.)	grisim	גרִיסִים (ז"ר)
flour	'kemaχ	קֶמַח (ז)
canned food	ʃimurim	שִימוּרִים (ז"ר)
cornflakes	ptitei 'tiras	פּתִיתֵי תִירָס (ז"ר)
honey	dvaʃ	דבַש (ז)
jam	riba	רִיבָּה (נ)
chewing gum	'mastik	מַסטִיק (ז)

53. Drinks

water	'mayim	מַיִם (ז"ר)
drinking water	mei ʃtiya	מֵי שתִייָה (ז"ר)
mineral water	'mayim mine'raliyim	מַיִם מִינֶרָלִיים (ז"ר)
still (adj)	lo mugaz	לֹא מוּגָז
carbonated (adj)	mugaz	מוּגָז
sparkling (adj)	mugaz	מוּגָז
ice	'keraχ	קֶרַח (ז)
with ice	im 'keraχ	עִם קֶרַח
non-alcoholic (adj)	natul alkohol	נָטוּל אַלכּוֹהוֹל
soft drink	maʃke kal	מַשקֶה קַל (ז)
refreshing drink	maʃke mera'anen	מַשקֶה מְרַעֲנֵן (ז)

lemonade	limo'nada	לִימוֹנָדָה (נ)
liquors	maʃka'ot χarifim	מַשְׁקָאוֹת חֲרִיפִים (ז"ר)
wine	'yayin	יַיִן (ז)
white wine	'yayin lavan	יַיִן לָבָן (ז)
red wine	'yayin adom	יַיִן אָדוֹם (ז)
liqueur	liker	לִיקֶר (ז)
champagne	ʃam'panya	שַׁמְפַּנְיָה (נ)
vermouth	'vermut	וֶרְמוּט (ז)
whiskey	'viski	וִיסְקִי (ז)
vodka	'vodka	וֹדְקָה (נ)
gin	dʒin	גִ׳ין (ז)
cognac	'konyak	קוֹנְיָאק (ז)
rum	rom	רוֹם (ז)
coffee	kafe	קָפֶה (ז)
black coffee	kafe ʃaχor	קָפֶה שָׁחוֹר (ז)
coffee with milk	kafe hafuχ	קָפֶה הָפוּךְ (ז)
cappuccino	kapu'tʃino	קָפוּצִ׳ינוֹ (ז)
instant coffee	kafe names	קָפֶה נָמֵס (ז)
milk	χalav	חָלָב (ז)
cocktail	kokteil	קוֹקְטֵיל (ז)
milkshake	'milkʃeik	מִילְקְשֵׁייק (ז)
juice	mits	מִיץ (ז)
tomato juice	mits agvaniyot	מִיץ עַגְבָנִיוֹת (ז)
orange juice	mits tapuzim	מִיץ תַפוּזִים (ז)
freshly squeezed juice	mits saχut	מִיץ סָחוּט (ז)
beer	'bira	בִּירָה (נ)
light beer	'bira bahira	בִּירָה בָּהִירָה (נ)
dark beer	'bira keha	בִּירָה כֵּהָה (נ)
tea	te	תֶה (ז)
black tea	te ʃaχor	תֶה שָׁחוֹר (ז)
green tea	te yarok	תֶה יָרוֹק (ז)

54. Vegetables

vegetables	yerakot	יְרָקוֹת (ז"ר)
greens	'yerek	יֶרֶק (ז)
tomato	agvaniya	עַגְבָנִייָה (נ)
cucumber	melafefon	מְלָפְפוֹן (ז)
carrot	'gezer	גֶזֶר (ז)
potato	ta'puaχ adama	תַפוּחַ אֲדָמָה (ז)
onion	batsal	בָּצָל (ז)
garlic	ʃum	שׁוּם (ז)

cabbage	kruv	כְּרוּב (ז)
cauliflower	kruvit	כְּרוּבִית (נ)
Brussels sprouts	kruv nitsanim	כְּרוּב נִצָּנִים (ז)
broccoli	'brokoli	בְּרוֹקוֹלִי (ז)
beetroot	'selek	סֶלֶק (ז)
eggplant	χatsil	חָצִיל (ז)
zucchini	kiʃu	קִישוּא (ז)
pumpkin	'dla'at	דְּלַעַת (נ)
turnip	'lefet	לֶפֶת (נ)
parsley	petro'zilya	פֶּטְרוֹזִילְיָה (נ)
dill	ʃamir	שָׁמִיר (ז)
lettuce	'χasa	חַסָּה (נ)
celery	'seleri	סֶלֶרִי (ז)
asparagus	aspa'ragos	אַסְפָּרָגוֹס (ז)
spinach	'tered	תֶּרֶד (ז)
pea	afuna	אֲפוּנָה (נ)
beans	pol	פּוֹל (ז)
corn (maize)	'tiras	תִּירָס (ז)
kidney bean	ʃu'it	שְׁעוּעִית (נ)
bell pepper	'pilpel	פִּלְפֵּל (ז)
radish	tsnonit	צְנוֹנִית (נ)
artichoke	artiʃok	אַרְטִישׁוֹק (ז)

55. Fruits. Nuts

fruit	pri	פְּרִי (ז)
apple	ta'puaχ	תַּפּוּחַ (ז)
pear	agas	אַגָּס (ז)
lemon	limon	לִימוֹן (ז)
orange	tapuz	תַּפּוּז (ז)
strawberry (garden ~)	tut sade	תּוּת שָׂדֶה (ז)
mandarin	klemen'tina	קְלֶמֶנְטִינָה (נ)
plum	ʃezif	שְׁזִיף (ז)
peach	afarsek	אֲפַרְסֵק (ז)
apricot	'miʃmeʃ	מִשְׁמֵשׁ (ז)
raspberry	'petel	פֶּטֶל (ז)
pineapple	'ananas	אֲנָנָס (ז)
banana	ba'nana	בַּנָנָה (נ)
watermelon	ava'tiaχ	אֲבַטִּיחַ (ז)
grape	anavim	עֲנָבִים (ז"ר)
sour cherry	duvdevan	דּוּבְדְּבָן (ז)
sweet cherry	gudgedan	גּוּדְגְּדָן (ז)
melon	melon	מֶלוֹן (ז)
grapefruit	eʃkolit	אֶשְׁכּוֹלִית (נ)

avocado	avo'kado	אֲבוֹקָדוֹ (ז)
papaya	pa'paya	פַּפָּאיָה (נ)
mango	'mango	מַנְגוֹ (ז)
pomegranate	rimon	רִימוֹן (ז)

redcurrant	dumdemanit aduma	דוּמְדְּמָנִית אֲדוֹמָה (נ)
blackcurrant	dumdemanit ʃxora	דוּמְדְּמָנִית שְׁחוֹרָה (נ)
gooseberry	xazarzar	חֲזַרְזַר (ז)
bilberry	uxmanit	אוּכְמָנִית (נ)
blackberry	'petel ʃaxor	פֶּטֶל שָׁחוֹר (ז)

raisin	tsimukim	צִימוּקִים (ז"ר)
fig	te'ena	תְּאֵנָה (נ)
date	tamar	תָּמָר (ז)

peanut	botnim	בּוֹטְנִים (ז"ר)
almond	ʃaked	שָׁקֵד (ז)
walnut	egoz 'melex	אֱגוֹז מֶלֶךְ (ז)
hazelnut	egoz ilsar	אֱגוֹז אִלְסָר (ז)
coconut	'kokus	קוֹקוּס (ז)
pistachios	'fistuk	פִּיסְטוּק (ז)

56. Bread. Candy

bakers' confectionery (pastry)	mutsrei kondi'torya	מוּצְרֵי קוֹנְדִיטוֹרְיָה (ז"ר)
bread	'lexem	לֶחֶם (ז)
cookies	ugiya	עוּגִיָּה (נ)

chocolate (n)	'ʃokolad	שׁוֹקוֹלָד (ז)
chocolate (as adj)	mi'ʃokolad	מְשׁוֹקוֹלָד
candy (wrapped)	sukariya	סוּכָּרִיָּה (נ)
cake (e.g., cupcake)	uga	עוּגָה (נ)
cake (e.g., birthday ~)	uga	עוּגָה (נ)

| pie (e.g., apple ~) | pai | פַּאי (ז) |
| filling (for cake, pie) | milui | מִילוּי (ז) |

jam (whole fruit jam)	riba	רִיבָּה (נ)
marmalade	marme'lada	מַרְמֶלָדָה (נ)
waffles	'vaflim	וַפְלִים (ז"ר)
ice-cream	'glida	גְלִידָה (נ)
pudding	'puding	פּוּדִינְג (ז)

57. Spices

| salt | 'melax | מֶלַח (ז) |
| salty (adj) | ma'luax | מָלוּחַ |

to salt (v)	leham'liaχ	לְהַמְלִיחַ
black pepper	'pilpel ʃaχor	פִּלְפֵּל שָׁחוֹר (ז)
red pepper (milled ~)	'pilpel adom	פִּלְפֵּל אָדֹם (ז)
mustard	χardal	חַרְדָּל (ז)
horseradish	χa'zeret	חֲזֶרֶת (נ)

condiment	'rotev	רוֹטֶב (ז)
spice	tavlin	תַּבְלִין (ז)
sauce	'rotev	רוֹטֶב (ז)
vinegar	'χomets	חֹמֶץ (ז)

anise	kamnon	כַּמְנוֹן (ז)
basil	reχan	רֵיחָן (ז)
cloves	tsi'poren	צִיפּוֹרֶן (ז)
ginger	'dʒindʒer	גִ׳ינגִ׳ר (ז)
coriander	'kusbara	כּוּסְבָּרָה (נ)
cinnamon	kinamon	קִינָמוֹן (ז)

sesame	'ʃumʃum	שׁוּמְשׁוֹם (ז)
bay leaf	ale dafna	עָלֵה דַפְנָה (ז)
paprika	'paprika	פַּפְּרִיקָה (נ)
caraway	'kimel	קִימֶל (ז)
saffron	ze'afran	זְעַפְרָן (ז)

PERSONAL INFORMATION. FAMILY

58. Personal information. Forms

name (first name)	ʃem	שֵׁם (ז)
surname (last name)	ʃem miʃpaχa	שֵׁם מִשְׁפָּחָה (ז)
date of birth	ta'ariχ leda	תַּאֲרִיךְ לֵידָה (ז)
place of birth	mekom leda	מְקוֹם לֵידָה (ז)
nationality	le'om	לְאוֹם (ז)
place of residence	mekom megurim	מְקוֹם מְגוּרִים (ז)
country	medina	מְדִינָה (נ)
profession (occupation)	mik'tso'a	מִקְצוֹעַ (ז)
gender, sex	min	מִין (ז)
height	'gova	גּוֹבַהּ (ז)
weight	miʃkal	מִשְׁקָל (ז)

59. Family members. Relatives

mother	em	אֵם (נ)
father	av	אָב (ז)
son	ben	בֵּן (ז)
daughter	bat	בַּת (נ)
younger daughter	habat haktana	הַבַּת הַקְּטַנָּה (נ)
younger son	haben hakatan	הַבֵּן הַקָּטָן (ז)
eldest daughter	habat habχora	הַבַּת הַבְּכוֹרָה (נ)
eldest son	haben habχor	הַבֵּן הַבְּכוֹר (ז)
brother	aχ	אָח (ז)
elder brother	aχ gadol	אָח גָּדוֹל (ז)
younger brother	aχ katan	אָח קָטָן (ז)
sister	aχot	אָחוֹת (נ)
elder sister	aχot gdola	אָחוֹת גְדוֹלָה (נ)
younger sister	aχot ktana	אָחוֹת קְטַנָּה (נ)
cousin (masc.)	ben dod	בֶּן דּוֹד (ז)
cousin (fem.)	bat 'doda	בַּת דּוֹדָה (נ)
mom, mommy	'ima	אִמָּא (נ)
dad, daddy	'aba	אַבָּא (ז)
parents	horim	הוֹרִים (ז"ר)
child	'yeled	יֶלֶד (ז)
children	yeladim	יְלָדִים (ז"ר)

grandmother	'savta	סַבְתָא (נ)
grandfather	'saba	סַבָּא (ז)
grandson	'neχed	נֶכֶד (ז)
granddaughter	neχda	נֶכְדָה (נ)
grandchildren	neχadim	נְכָדִים (ז״ר)
uncle	dod	דוֹד (ז)
aunt	'doda	דוֹדָה (נ)
nephew	aχyan	אַחְיָין (ז)
niece	aχyanit	אַחְיָינִית (נ)

mother-in-law (wife's mother)	χamot	חָמוֹת (נ)
father-in-law (husband's father)	χam	חָם (ז)
son-in-law (daughter's husband)	χatan	חָתָן (ז)
stepmother	em χoreget	אֵם חוֹרֶגֶת (נ)
stepfather	av χoreg	אָב חוֹרֵג (ז)

infant	tinok	תִינוֹק (ז)
baby (infant)	tinok	תִינוֹק (ז)
little boy, kid	pa'ot	פָּעוֹט (ז)
wife	iʃa	אִשָה (נ)
husband	'ba'al	בַּעַל (ז)
spouse (husband)	ben zug	בֶּן זוּג (ז)
spouse (wife)	bat zug	בַּת זוּג (נ)

married (masc.)	nasui	נָשׂוּי
married (fem.)	nesu'a	נְשׂוּאָה
single (unmarried)	ravak	רַוָוק
bachelor	ravak	רַוָוק (ז)
divorced (masc.)	garuʃ	גָרוּש
widow	almana	אַלְמָנָה (נ)
widower	alman	אַלְמָן (ז)

relative	karov miʃpaχa	קָרוֹב מִשְפָּחָה (ז)
close relative	karov miʃpaχa	קָרוֹב מִשְפָּחָה (ז)
distant relative	karov raχok	קָרוֹב רָחוֹק (ז)
relatives	krovei miʃpaχa	קְרוֹבֵי מִשְפָּחָה (ז״ר)

orphan (boy)	yatom	יָתוֹם (ז)
orphan (girl)	yetoma	יְתוֹמָה (נ)
guardian (of a minor)	apo'tropos	אַפּוֹטְרוֹפּוֹס (ז)
to adopt (a boy)	le'amets	לְאַמֵץ
to adopt (a girl)	le'amets	לְאַמֵץ

60. Friends. Coworkers

| friend (masc.) | χaver | חָבֵר (ז) |
| friend (fem.) | χavera | חָבֵרָה (נ) |

friendship	yedidut	יְדִידוּת (נ)
to be friends	lihyot yadidim	לִהְיוֹת יָדִידִים
buddy (masc.)	xaver	חָבֵר (ז)
buddy (fem.)	xavera	חֲבֵרָה (נ)
partner	ʃutaf	שׁוּתָף (ז)
chief (boss)	menahel, roʃ	מְנַהֵל (ז), רֹאשׁ (ז)
superior (n)	memune	מְמוּנָה (ז)
owner, proprietor	be'alim	בְּעָלִים (ז)
subordinate (n)	kafuf le	כָּפוּף ל (ז)
colleague	amit	עָמִית (ז)
acquaintance (person)	makar	מַכָּר (ז)
fellow traveler	ben levaya	בֶּן לְוָיָה (ז)
classmate	xaver lekita	חָבֵר לְכִּיתָה (ז)
neighbor (masc.)	ʃaxen	שָׁכֵן (ז)
neighbor (fem.)	ʃxena	שׁכֵנָה (נ)
neighbors	ʃxenim	שׁכֵנִים (ז"ר)

HUMAN BODY. MEDICINE

61. Head

head	roʃ	רֹאש (ז)
face	panim	פָּנִים (ז"ר)
nose	af	אַף (ז)
mouth	pe	פֶּה (ז)

eye	'ayin	עַיִן (נ)
eyes	ei'nayim	עֵינַיִים (נ"ר)
pupil	iʃon	אִישׁוֹן (ז)
eyebrow	gaba	גַבָּה (נ)
eyelash	ris	רִיס (ז)
eyelid	af'af	עַפעַף (ז)

tongue	laʃon	לָשׁוֹן (נ)
tooth	ʃen	שֵׁן (נ)
lips	sfa'tayim	שֹׂפָתַיִים (נ"ר)
cheekbones	atsamot leχa'yayim	עַצמוֹת לְחָיַיִם (נ"ר)
gum	χani'χayim	חֲנִיכַיִים (ז"ר)
palate	χeχ	חֵך (ז)

nostrils	neχi'rayim	נְחִירַיִים (ז"ר)
chin	santer	סַנטֵר (ז)
jaw	'leset	לֶסֶת (נ)
cheek	'leχi	לְחִי (נ)

forehead	'metsaχ	מֵצַח (ז)
temple	raka	רַקָה (נ)
ear	'ozen	אוֹזֶן (נ)
back of the head	'oref	עוֹרֶף (ז)
neck	tsavar	צַוָאר (ז)
throat	garon	גָרוֹן (ז)

hair	se'ar	שֵׂיעָר (ז)
hairstyle	tis'roket	תִסרוֹקֶת (נ)
haircut	tis'poret	תִספּוֹרֶת (נ)
wig	pe'a	פֵּאָה (נ)

mustache	safam	שָׂפָם (ז)
beard	zakan	זָקָן (ז)
to have (a beard, etc.)	legadel	לְגַדֵל
braid	tsama	צַמָה (נ)
sideburns	pe'ot leχa'yayim	פֵּאוֹת לְחָיַיִם (נ"ר)
red-haired (adj)	'dʒindʒi	גִ'ינגִ'י

gray (hair)	kasuf	כָּסוּף
bald (adj)	ke'reaχ	קֵירֵחַ
bald patch	ka'raχat	קָרַחַת (נ)
ponytail	'kuku	קוּקוּ (ז)
bangs	'poni	פּוֹנִי (ז)

62. Human body

hand	kaf yad	כַּף יָד (נ)
arm	yad	יָד (נ)
finger	'etsba	אֶצְבַּע (נ)
toe	'bohen	בּוֹהֶן (נ)
thumb	agudal	אֲגוּדָל (ז)
little finger	'zeret	זֶרֶת (נ)
nail	tsi'poren	צִיפּוֹרֶן (נ)
fist	egrof	אֶגְרוֹף (ז)
palm	kaf yad	כַּף יָד (נ)
wrist	'ʃoreʃ kaf hayad	שׁוֹרֶשׁ כַּף הַיָד (ז)
forearm	ama	אַמָה (נ)
elbow	marpek	מַרְפֵּק (ז)
shoulder	katef	כָּתֵף (נ)
leg	'regel	רֶגֶל (נ)
foot	kaf 'regel	כַּף רֶגֶל (נ)
knee	'bereχ	בֶּרֶךְ (נ)
calf (part of leg)	ʃok	שׁוֹק (נ)
hip	yareχ	יָרֵךְ (ז)
heel	akev	עָקֵב (ז)
body	guf	גוּף (ז)
stomach	'beten	בֶּטֶן (נ)
chest	χaze	חָזֶה (ז)
breast	ʃad	שַׁד (ז)
flank	tsad	צַד (ז)
back	gav	גַב (ז)
lower back	mot'nayim	מוֹתְנַיִים (ז"ר)
waist	'talya	טַלְיָה (נ)
navel (belly button)	tabur	טַבּוּר (ז)
buttocks	aχo'rayim	אֲחוֹרַיִים (ז"ר)
bottom	yaʃvan	יַשְׁבָן (ז)
beauty mark	nekudat χen	נְקוּדַת חֵן (נ)
birthmark (café au lait spot)	'ketem leida	כֶּתֶם לֵידָה (ז)
tattoo	ka'a'ku'a	קַעֲקוּעַ (ז)
scar	tsa'leket	צַלֶּקֶת (נ)

63. Diseases

sickness	maxala	מַחֲלָה (נ)
to be sick	lihyot xole	לִהְיוֹת חוֹלֶה
health	bri'ut	בְּרִיאוּת (נ)
runny nose (coryza)	na'zelet	נַזֶּלֶת (נ)
tonsillitis	da'leket ʃkedim	דַּלֶּקֶת שְׁקֵדִים (נ)
cold (illness)	hitstanenut	הִצְטַנְּנוּת (נ)
to catch a cold	lehitstanen	לְהִצְטַנֵּן
bronchitis	bron'xitis	בְּרוֹנְכִיטִיס (ז)
pneumonia	da'leket re'ot	דַּלֶּקֶת רֵיאוֹת (נ)
flu, influenza	ʃa'pa'at	שַׁפַּעַת (נ)
nearsighted (adj)	ktsar re'iya	קְצַר רְאִיָּה
farsighted (adj)	rexok re'iya	רְחוֹק־רְאִיָּה
strabismus (crossed eyes)	pzila	פְּזִילָה (נ)
cross-eyed (adj)	pozel	פּוֹזֵל
cataract	katarakt	קָטָרַקְט (ז)
glaucoma	gla'u'koma	גְּלָאוּקוֹמָה (נ)
stroke	ʃavats moxi	שְׁבָץ מוֹחִי (ז)
heart attack	hetkef lev	הֶתְקֵף לֵב (ז)
myocardial infarction	'otem ʃrir halev	אוֹטֶם שְׁרִיר הַלֵּב (ז)
paralysis	ʃituk	שִׁיתוּק (ז)
to paralyze (vt)	leʃatek	לְשַׁתֵּק
allergy	a'lergya	אָלֶרְגְּיָה (נ)
asthma	'astma, ka'tseret	אַסְתְמָה, קַצֶּרֶת (נ)
diabetes	su'keret	סֻכֶּרֶת (נ)
toothache	ke'ev ʃi'nayim	כְּאֵב שִׁינַיִים (ז)
caries	a'ʃeʃet	עַשֶּׁשֶׁת (נ)
diarrhea	ʃilʃul	שִׁלְשׁוּל (ז)
constipation	atsirut	עֲצִירוּת (נ)
stomach upset	kilkul keiva	קִלְקוּל קֵיבָה (ז)
food poisoning	har'alat mazon	הַרְעָלַת מָזוֹן (נ)
to get food poisoning	laxatof har'alat mazon	לַחְטוֹף הַרְעָלַת מָזוֹן
arthritis	da'leket mifrakim	דַּלֶּקֶת מִפְרָקִים (נ)
rickets	ra'kexet	רַכֶּכֶת (נ)
rheumatism	ʃigaron	שִׁיגָּרוֹן (ז)
atherosclerosis	ar'teryo skle'rosis	אַרְטֶרְיוֹ־סְקְלֶרוֹסִיס (ז)
gastritis	da'leket keiva	דַּלֶּקֶת קֵיבָה (נ)
appendicitis	da'leket toseftan	דַּלֶּקֶת תּוֹסֶפְתָּן (נ)
cholecystitis	da'leket kis hamara	דַּלֶּקֶת כִּיס הַמָּרָה (נ)
ulcer	'ulkus, kiv	אוּלְקוּס, כִּיב (ז)
measles	xa'tsevet	חַצֶּבֶת (נ)

rubella (German measles)	a'demet	אַדֶּמֶת (נ)
jaundice	tsa'hevet	צַהֶבֶת (נ)
hepatitis	da'leket kaved	דַּלֶּקֶת כָּבֵד (נ)
schizophrenia	sχizo'frenya	סְכִיזוֹפְרֶנְיָה (נ)
rabies (hydrophobia)	ka'levet	כַּלֶּבֶת (נ)
neurosis	noi'roza	נוֹירוֹזָה (נ)
concussion	za'a'zu'a 'moaχ	זַעֲזוּעַ מוֹחַ (ז)
cancer	sartan	סַרְטָן (ז)
sclerosis	ta'refet	טָרֶשֶׁת (נ)
multiple sclerosis	ta'refet nefotsa	טָרֶשֶׁת נְפוֹצָה (נ)
alcoholism	alkoholizm	אַלְכּוֹהוֹלִיזֶם (ז)
alcoholic (n)	alkoholist	אַלְכּוֹהוֹלִיסְט (ז)
syphilis	a'gevet	עַגֶּבֶת (נ)
AIDS	eids	אָיְידְס (ז)
tumor	gidul	גִּידוּל (ז)
malignant (adj)	mam'ir	מַמְאִיר
benign (adj)	ʃapir	שַׁפִּיר
fever	ka'daχat	קַדַּחַת (נ)
malaria	ma'larya	מָלַרְיָה (נ)
gangrene	gan'grena	גַּנְגְּרֶנָה (נ)
seasickness	maχalat yam	מַחֲלַת יָם (נ)
epilepsy	maχalat hanefila	מַחֲלַת הַנְּפִילָה (נ)
epidemic	magefa	מַגֵּיפָה (נ)
typhus	'tifus	טִיפוּס (ז)
tuberculosis	ʃa'χefet	שַׁחֶפֶת (נ)
cholera	ko'lera	כּוֹלֵרָה (נ)
plague (bubonic ~)	davar	דֶּבֶר (ז)

64. Symptoms. Treatments. Part 1

symptom	simptom	סִימְפְּטוֹם (ז)
temperature	χom	חוֹם (ז)
high temperature (fever)	χom ga'voha	חוֹם גָּבוֹהַּ (ז)
pulse	'dofek	דּוֹפֶק (ז)
dizziness (vertigo)	sχar'χoret	סְחַרְחוֹרֶת (נ)
hot (adj)	χam	חַם
shivering	tsmar'moret	צְמַרְמוֹרֶת (נ)
pale (e.g., ~ face)	χiver	חִיוֵּר
cough	ʃi'ul	שִׁיעוּל (ז)
to cough (vi)	lehiʃta'el	לְהִשְׁתַּעֵל
to sneeze (vi)	lehit'ateʃ	לְהִתְעַטֵּשׁ
faint	ilafon	עִילָפוֹן (ז)

to faint (vi)	lehit'alef	לְהִתעַלֵף
bruise (hématome)	xabura	חַבּוּרָה (נ)
bump (lump)	blita	בּלִיטָה (נ)
to bang (bump)	lekabel maka	לְקַבֵּל מַכָּה
contusion (bruise)	maka	מַכָּה (נ)
to get a bruise	lekabel maka	לְקַבֵּל מַכָּה
to limp (vi)	lits'lo'a	לְצלוֹעַ
dislocation	'neka	נֶקַע (ז)
to dislocate (vt)	lin'ko'a	לִנקוֹעַ
fracture	'ʃever	שֶבֶר (ז)
to have a fracture	liʃbor	לִשבּוֹר
cut (e.g., paper ~)	xatax	חָתָך (ז)
to cut oneself	lehixatex	לְהֵיחָתֵך
bleeding	dimum	דִימוּם (ז)
burn (injury)	kviya	כּוְוִיָה (נ)
to get burned	laxatof kviya	לַחֲטוֹף כּוְוִיָה
to prick (vt)	lidkor	לִדקוֹר
to prick oneself	lehidaker	לְהִידָקֵר
to injure (vt)	lif'tso'a	לִפצוֹעַ
injury	ptsi'a	פּצִיעָה (נ)
wound	'petsa	פֶּצַע (ז)
trauma	'tra'uma	טרָאוּמָה (נ)
to be delirious	lahazot	לַהֲזוֹת
to stutter (vi)	legamgem	לְגַמגֵם
sunstroke	makat 'ʃemeʃ	מַכַּת שֶמֶש (נ)

65. Symptoms. Treatments. Part 2

pain, ache	ke'ev	כְּאֵב (ז)
splinter (in foot, etc.)	kots	קוֹץ (ז)
sweat (perspiration)	ze'a	זֵיעָה (נ)
to sweat (perspire)	leha'zi'a	לְהַזִיעַ
vomiting	haka'a	הֲקָאָה (נ)
convulsions	pirkusim	פִּירפּוּסִים (ז"ר)
pregnant (adj)	hara	הָרָה
to be born	lehivaled	לְהִיוָולֵד
delivery, labor	leda	לֵידָה (נ)
to deliver (~ a baby)	la'ledet	לָלֶדֶת
abortion	hapala	הַפָּלָה (נ)
breathing, respiration	neʃima	נְשִימָה (נ)
in-breath (inhalation)	ʃe'ifa	שְאִיפָה (נ)
out-breath (exhalation)	neʃifa	נְשִיפָה (נ)

| to exhale (breathe out) | linʃof | לִנְשׁוֹף |
| to inhale (vi) | liʃʼof | לִשְׁאוֹף |

disabled person	naxe	נָכֶה (ז)
cripple	naxe	נָכֶה (ז)
drug addict	narkoman	נַרְקוֹמָן (ז)

deaf (adj)	xereʃ	חֵירֵשׁ
mute (adj)	ilem	אִילֵם
deaf mute (adj)	xereʃ-ilem	חֵירֵשׁ־אִילֵם

mad, insane (adj)	meʃuga	מְשׁוּגָע
madman (demented person)	meʃuga	מְשׁוּגָע (ז)
madwoman	meʃuʼgaʼat	מְשׁוּגַעַת (נ)
to go insane	lehiʃtaʼgeʼa	לְהִשְׁתַּגֵּעַ

gene	gen	גֵּן (ז)
immunity	xasinut	חֲסִינוּת (נ)
hereditary (adj)	toraʃti	תּוֹרַשְׁתִּי
congenital (adj)	mulad	מוֹלָד

virus	ʼvirus	וִירוּס (ז)
microbe	xaidak	חַיְדָּק (ז)
bacterium	bakʼterya	בַּקְטֶרְיָה (נ)
infection	zihum	זִיהוּם (ז)

66. Symptoms. Treatments. Part 3

| hospital | beit xolim | בֵּית חוֹלִים (ז) |
| patient | metupal | מְטוּפָּל (ז) |

diagnosis	avxana	אַבְחָנָה (נ)
cure	ripui	רִיפּוּי (ז)
medical treatment	tipul refuʼi	טִיפּוּל רְפוּאִי (ז)
to get treatment	lekabel tipul	לְקַבֵּל טִיפּוּל
to treat (~ a patient)	letapel be...	לְטַפֵּל בְּ...
to nurse (look after)	letapel be...	לְטַפֵּל בְּ...
care (nursing ~)	tipul	טִיפּוּל (ז)

operation, surgery	niʼtuax	נִיתּוּחַ (ז)
to bandage (head, limb)	laxboʃ	לַחְבּוֹשׁ
bandaging	xaviʃa	חֲבִישָׁה (נ)

vaccination	xisun	חִיסּוּן (ז)
to vaccinate (vt)	lexasen	לְחַסֵּן
injection, shot	zrika	זְרִיקָה (נ)
to give an injection	lehazrik	לְהַזְרִיק
attack	hetkef	הַתְקֵף (ז)
amputation	ktiʼa	קְטִיעָה (נ)

to amputate (vt)	lik'to'a	לִקְטוֹעַ
coma	tar'demet	תַּרְדֶּמֶת (נ)
to be in a coma	lihyot betar'demet	לִהְיוֹת בְּתַרְדֶּמֶת
intensive care	tipul nimrats	טִיפּוּל נִמְרָץ (ז)
to recover (~ from flu)	lehaxlim	לְהַחְלִים
condition (patient's ~)	matsav	מַצָּב (ז)
consciousness	hakara	הַכָּרָה (נ)
memory (faculty)	zikaron	זִיכָּרוֹן (ז)
to pull out (tooth)	la'akor	לַעֲקוֹר
filling	stima	סְתִימָה (נ)
to fill (a tooth)	la'asot stima	לַעֲשׂוֹת סְתִימָה
hypnosis	hip'noza	הִיפְּנוֹזָה (נ)
to hypnotize (vt)	lehapnet	לְהַפְנֵט

67. Medicine. Drugs. Accessories

medicine, drug	trufa	תְּרוּפָה (נ)
remedy	trufa	תְּרוּפָה (נ)
to prescribe (vt)	lirſom	לִרְשׁוֹם
prescription	mirſam	מִרְשָׁם (ז)
tablet, pill	kadur	כַּדּוּר (ז)
ointment	miſxa	מִשְׁחָה (נ)
ampule	'ampula	אַמְפּוּלָה (נ)
mixture	ta'a'rovet	תַּעֲרוֹבֶת (נ)
syrup	sirop	סִירוֹפּ (ז)
pill	gluya	גְלוּיָה (נ)
powder	avka	אַבְקָה (נ)
gauze bandage	tax'boſet 'gaza	תַּחְבּוֹשֶׁת גָּאזָה (נ)
cotton wool	'tsemer 'gefen	צֶמֶר גֶּפֶן (ז)
iodine	yod	יוֹד (ז)
Band-Aid	'plaster	פְּלַסְטֶר (ז)
eyedropper	taf'tefet	טַפְטֶפֶת (נ)
thermometer	madxom	מַדְחוֹם (ז)
syringe	mazrek	מַזְרֵק (ז)
wheelchair	kise galgalim	כִּיסֵא גַלְגַלִים (ז)
crutches	ka'bayim	קַבַּיִים (ז"ר)
painkiller	meſakex ke'evim	מְשַׁכֵּךְ כְּאֵבִים (ז)
laxative	trufa meſal'ſelet	תְּרוּפָה מְשַׁלְשֶׁלֶת (נ)
spirits (ethanol)	'kohal	כּוֹהַל (ז)
medicinal herbs	isvei marpe	עִשְׂבֵי מַרְפֵּא (ז"ר)
herbal (~ tea)	ſel asavim	שֶׁל עֲשָׂבִים

APARTMENT

68. Apartment

apartment	dira	דִירָה (נ)
room	'xeder	חֶדֶר (ז)
bedroom	xadar ʃena	חֲדַר שֵינָה (ז)
dining room	pinat 'oxel	פִּינַת אוֹכֶל (נ)
living room	salon	סָלוֹן (ז)
study (home office)	xadar avoda	חֲדַר עֲבוֹדָה (ז)
entry room	prozdor	פרוֹזדוֹר (ז)
bathroom (room with a bath or shower)	xadar am'batya	חֲדַר אַמבַּטיָה (ז)
half bath	ʃerutim	שֵירוּתִים (ז"ר)
ceiling	tikra	תִקרָה (נ)
floor	ritspa	רִצפָּה (נ)
corner	pina	פִּינָה (נ)

69. Furniture. Interior

furniture	rehitim	רָהִיטִים (ז"ר)
table	ʃulxan	שוּלחָן (ז)
chair	kise	כִּסֵא (ז)
bed	mita	מִיטָה (נ)
couch, sofa	sapa	סַפָּה (נ)
armchair	kursa	כּוּרסָה (נ)
bookcase	aron sfarim	אָרוֹן סְפָרִים (ז)
shelf	madaf	מַדָף (ז)
wardrobe	aron bgadim	אָרוֹן בּגָדִים (ז)
coat rack (wall-mounted ~)	mitle	מִתלֶה (ז)
coat stand	mitle	מִתלֶה (ז)
bureau, dresser	ʃida	שִידָה (נ)
coffee table	ʃulxan itonim	שוּלחַן עִיתוֹנִים (ז)
mirror	mar'a	מַראָה (נ)
carpet	ʃa'tiax	שָטִיחַ (ז)
rug, small carpet	ʃa'tiax	שָטִיחַ (ז)
fireplace	ax	אָח (נ)
candle	ner	נֵר (ז)

candlestick	pamot	פָמוֹט (ז)
drapes	vilonot	וִילוֹנוֹת (ז״ר)
wallpaper	tapet	טַפֶט (ז)
blinds (jalousie)	trisim	תְרִיסִים (ז״ר)

table lamp	menorat ʃulxan	מְנוֹרַת שׁוּלחָן (נ)
wall lamp (sconce)	menorat kir	מְנוֹרַת קִיר (נ)
floor lamp	menora o'medet	מְנוֹרָה עוֹמֶדֶת (נ)
chandelier	niv'reʃet	נִברֶשֶׁת (נ)

leg (of chair, table)	'regel	רֶגֶל (נ)
armrest	miʃ'enet yad	מִשׁעֶנֶת יָד (נ)
back (backrest)	miʃ'enet	מִשׁעֶנֶת (נ)
drawer	megera	מְגֵירָה (נ)

70. Bedding

bedclothes	matsa'im	מַצָעִים (ז״ר)
pillow	karit	כָּרִית (נ)
pillowcase	tsipit	צִיפִּית (נ)
duvet, comforter	smixa	שֹׁמִיכָה (נ)
sheet	sadin	סָדִין (ז)
bedspread	kisui mita	כִּיסוּי מִיטָה (ז)

71. Kitchen

kitchen	mitbax	מִטבָּח (ז)
gas	gaz	גָז (ז)
gas stove (range)	tanur gaz	תַנוּר גָז (ז)
electric stove	tanur xaʃmali	תַנוּר חַשׁמַלִי (ז)
oven	tanur afiya	תַנוּר אָפִיָה (ז)
microwave oven	mikrogal	מִיקרוֹגַל (ז)

refrigerator	mekarer	מְקָרֵר (ז)
freezer	makpi	מַקפִּיא (ז)
dishwasher	me'diax kelim	מֵדִיחַ כֵּלִים (ז)

meat grinder	matxenat basar	מַטחֲנַת בָּשָׂר (נ)
juicer	masxeta	מַסחֵטָה (נ)
toaster	'toster	טוֹסטֶר (ז)
mixer	'mikser	מִיקסֶר (ז)

coffee machine	mexonat kafe	מְכוֹנַת קָפֶה (נ)
coffee pot	findʒan	פִינג׳אן (ז)
coffee grinder	matxenat kafe	מַטחֲנַת קָפֶה (נ)

| kettle | kumkum | קוּמקוּם (ז) |
| teapot | kumkum | קוּמקוּם (ז) |

lid	miχse	מְכֶסֶה (ז)
tea strainer	mis'nenet te	מְסַנֶּנֶת תֵּה (נ)
spoon	kaf	כַּף (נ)
teaspoon	kapit	כַּפִּית (נ)
soup spoon	kaf	כַּף (נ)
fork	mazleg	מַזְלֵג (ז)
knife	sakin	סַכִּין (ז, נ)
tableware (dishes)	kelim	כֵּלִים (ז"ר)
plate (dinner ~)	tsa'laχat	צַלַּחַת (נ)
saucer	taχtit	תַּחְתִּית (נ)
shot glass	kosit	כּוֹסִית (נ)
glass (tumbler)	kos	כּוֹס (נ)
cup	'sefel	סֵפֶל (ז)
sugar bowl	mis'keret	מִסְכֶּרֶת (נ)
salt shaker	milχiya	מִלְחִיָּה (נ)
pepper shaker	pilpeliya	פִּלְפְּלִיָּה (נ)
butter dish	maχame'a	מַחְמָאָה (נ)
stock pot (soup pot)	sir	סִיר (ז)
frying pan (skillet)	maχvat	מַחְבַת (נ)
ladle	tarvad	תַּרְוָד (ז)
colander	mis'nenet	מְסַנֶּנֶת (נ)
tray (serving ~)	magaʃ	מַגָּשׁ (ז)
bottle	bakbuk	בַּקְבּוּק (ז)
jar (glass)	tsin'tsenet	צִנְצֶנֶת (נ)
can	paχit	פַּחִית (נ)
bottle opener	potχan bakbukim	פּוֹתְחָן בַּקְבּוּקִים (ז)
can opener	potχan kufsa'ot	פּוֹתְחָן קוּפְסָאוֹת (ז)
corkscrew	maχlets	מַחְלֵץ (ז)
filter	'filter	פִּילְטֶר (ז)
to filter (vt)	lesanen	לְסַנֵּן
trash, garbage (food waste, etc.)	'zevel	זֶבֶל (ז)
trash can (kitchen ~)	paχ 'zevel	פַּח זֶבֶל (ז)

72. Bathroom

bathroom	χadar am'batya	חֲדַר אַמְבַּטְיָה (ז)
water	'mayim	מַיִם (ז"ר)
faucet	'berez	בֶּרֶז (ז)
hot water	'mayim χamim	מַיִם חַמִּים (ז"ר)
cold water	'mayim karim	מַיִם קָרִים (ז"ר)
toothpaste	miʃχat ʃi'nayim	מִשְׁחַת שִׁינַיִם (נ)

to brush one's teeth	letsax'tseax ʃi'nayim	לְצַחְצֵחַ שִׁינַיִים
toothbrush	miv'reʃet ʃi'nayim	מִבְרֶשֶׁת שִׁינַיִים (נ)
to shave (vi)	lehitga'leax	לְהִתְגַּלֵּחַ
shaving foam	'ketsef gi'luax	קֶצֶף גִּילוּחַ (ז)
razor	'ta'ar	תַּעַר (ז)
to wash (one's hands, etc.)	liʃtof	לִשְׁטוֹף
to take a bath	lehitraxets	לְהִתְרַחֵץ
shower	mik'laxat	מִקְלַחַת (נ)
to take a shower	lehitka'leax	לְהִתְקַלֵּחַ
bathtub	am'batya	אַמְבַּטְיָה (נ)
toilet (toilet bowl)	asla	אַסְלָה (נ)
sink (washbasin)	kiyor	כִּיּוֹר (ז)
soap	sabon	סַבּוֹן (ז)
soap dish	saboniya	סַבּוֹנִיָּיה (נ)
sponge	sfog 'lifa	סְפוֹג לִיפָה (ז)
shampoo	ʃampu	שַׁמְפּוּ (ז)
towel	ma'gevet	מַגֶּבֶת (נ)
bathrobe	xaluk raxatsa	חָלוּק רַחְצָה (ז)
laundry (process)	kvisa	כְּבִיסָה (נ)
washing machine	mexonat kvisa	מְכוֹנַת כְּבִיסָה (נ)
to do the laundry	lexabes	לְכַבֵּס
laundry detergent	avkat kvisa	אַבְקַת כְּבִיסָה (נ)

73. Household appliances

TV set	tele'vizya	טֶלֶוִוִיזְיָה (נ)
tape recorder	teip	טֵייפּ (ז)
VCR (video recorder)	maxʃir 'vide'o	מַכְשִׁיר וִידֵאוֹ (ז)
radio	'radyo	רַדְיוֹ (ז)
player (CD, MP3, etc.)	nagan	נַגָּן (ז)
video projector	makren	מַקְרֵן (ז)
home movie theater	kol'no'a beiti	קוֹלְנוֹעַ בֵּיתִי (ז)
DVD player	nagan dividi	נַגָּן DVD (ז)
amplifier	magber	מַגְבֵּר (ז)
video game console	maxʃir plei'steiʃen	מַכְשִׁיר פְּלֵייסְטֵיישֶׁן (ז)
video camera	matslemat 'vide'o	מַצְלֵמַת וִידֵאוֹ (נ)
camera (photo)	matslema	מַצְלֵמָה (נ)
digital camera	matslema digi'talit	מַצְלֵמָה דִיגִיטָלִית (נ)
vacuum cleaner	ʃo'ev avak	שׁוֹאֵב אָבָק (ז)
iron (e.g., steam ~)	maghets	מַגְהֵץ (ז)
ironing board	'kereʃ gihuts	קֶרֶשׁ גִּיהוּץ (ז)

telephone	'telefon	טֶלֶפוֹן (ז)
cell phone	'telefon nayad	טֶלֶפוֹן נַיָיד (ז)
typewriter	meχonat ktiva	מְכוֹנַת כְּתִיבָה (נ)
sewing machine	meχonat tfira	מְכוֹנַת תְּפִירָה (נ)

microphone	mikrofon	מִיקרוֹפוֹן (ז)
headphones	ozniyot	אוֹזנִיוֹת (נ"ר)
remote control (TV)	'ʃelet	שֶׁלֶט (ז)

CD, compact disc	taklitor	תַקלִיטוֹר (ז)
cassette, tape	ka'letet	קַלֶטֶת (נ)
vinyl record	taklit	תַקלִיט (ז)

THE EARTH. WEATHER

74. Outer space

space	χalal	חָלָל (ז)
space (as adj)	ʃel χalal	שֶׁל חָלָל
outer space	χalal χitson	חָלָל חִיצוֹן (ז)
world	olam	עוֹלָם (ז)
universe	yekum	יְקוּם (ז)
galaxy	ga'laksya	גָלַקסיָה (נ)
star	koχav	כּוֹכָב (ז)
constellation	tsvir koχavim	צבִיר כּוֹכָבִים (ז)
planet	koχav 'leχet	כּוֹכָב לֶכֶת (ז)
satellite	lavyan	לַוויָן (ז)
meteorite	mete'orit	מֶטָאוֹרִיט (ז)
comet	koχav ʃavit	כּוֹכָב שָׁבִיט (ז)
asteroid	aste'ro'id	אַסטֶרוֹאִיד (ז)
orbit	maslul	מַסלוּל (ז)
to revolve	lesovev	לְסוֹבֵב
(~ around the Earth)		
atmosphere	atmos'fera	אַטמוֹספֶרָה (נ)
the Sun	'ʃemeʃ	שֶׁמֶשׁ (נ)
solar system	ma'a'reχet ha'ʃemeʃ	מַעֲרֶכֶת הַשֶׁמֶשׁ (נ)
solar eclipse	likui χama	לִיקוּי חַמָה (ז)
the Earth	kadur ha''arets	כַּדוּר הָאָרֶץ (ז)
the Moon	ya'reaχ	יָרֵחַ (ז)
Mars	ma'adim	מַאֲדִים (ז)
Venus	'noga	נוֹגַה (ז)
Jupiter	'tsedek	צֶדֶק (ז)
Saturn	ʃabtai	שַׁבּתַאי (ז)
Mercury	koχav χama	כּוֹכָב חַמָה (ז)
Uranus	u'ranus	אוֹרָנוּס (ז)
Neptune	neptun	נֶפטוּן (ז)
Pluto	'pluto	פּלוּטוֹ (ז)
Milky Way	ʃvil haχalav	שׁבִיל הֶחָלָב (ז)
Great Bear (Ursa Major)	duba gdola	דוּבָּה גדוֹלָה (נ)
North Star	koχav hatsafon	כּוֹכָב הַצָפוֹן (ז)
Martian	toʃav ma'adim	תוֹשָׁב מַאֲדִים (ז)

extraterrestrial (n)	xutsan	חוֹצָן (ז)
alien	xaizar	חַייזָר (ז)
flying saucer	tsa'laxat me'o'fefet	צַלַחַת מְעוֹפֶפֶת (נ)
spaceship	xalalit	חָלָלִית (נ)
space station	taxanat xalal	תַחֲנַת חָלָל (נ)
blast-off	hamra'a	הַמרָאָה (נ)
engine	ma'no'a	מָנוֹעַ (ז)
nozzle	nexir	נְחִיר (ז)
fuel	'delek	דֶלֶק (ז)
cockpit, flight deck	'kokpit	קוֹקפִּיט (ז)
antenna	an'tena	אַנטֶנָה (נ)
porthole	eʃnav	אֶשנָב (ז)
solar panel	'luax so'lari	לוּחַ סוֹלָרִי (ז)
spacesuit	xalifat xalal	חֲלִיפַת חָלָל (נ)
weightlessness	'xoser miʃkal	חוֹסֶר מִשקָל (ז)
oxygen	xamtsan	חַמצָן (ז)
docking (in space)	agina	עֲגִינָה (נ)
to dock (vi, vt)	la'agon	לַעֲגוֹן
observatory	mitspe koxavim	מִצפֶּה כּוֹכָבִים (ז)
telescope	teleskop	טֶלֶסקוֹפּ (ז)
to observe (vt)	litspot, lehaʃkif	לִצפּוֹת, לְהַשקִיף
to explore (vt)	laxkor	לַחקוֹר

75. The Earth

the Earth	kadur ha''arets	כַּדוּר הָאָרֶץ (ז)
the globe (the Earth)	kadur ha''arets	כַּדוּר הָאָרֶץ (ז)
planet	koxav 'lexet	כּוֹכָב לֶכֶת (ז)
atmosphere	atmos'fera	אַטמוֹספֶרָה (נ)
geography	ge'o'grafya	גִיאוֹגרַפיָה (נ)
nature	'teva	טֶבַע (ז)
globe (table ~)	'globus	גלוֹבּוּס (ז)
map	mapa	מַפָּה (נ)
atlas	'atlas	אַטלָס (ז)
Europe	ei'ropa	אֵירוֹפָּה (נ)
Asia	'asya	אַסיָה (נ)
Africa	'afrika	אַפרִיקָה (נ)
Australia	ost'ralya	אוֹסטרַליָה (נ)
America	a'merika	אָמֶרִיקָה (נ)
North America	a'merika hatsfonit	אָמֶרִיקָה הַצפוֹנִית (נ)

South America	a'merika hadromit	אָמֶרִיקָה הַדְרוֹמִית (נ)
Antarctica	ya'beʃet an'tarktika	יַבֶּשֶׁת אַנְטָארְקְטִיקָה (נ)
the Arctic	'arktika	אַרְקְטִיקָה (נ)

76. Cardinal directions

north	tsafon	צָפוֹן (ז)
to the north	tsa'fona	צָפוֹנָה
in the north	batsafon	בַּצָּפוֹן
northern (adj)	tsfoni	צְפוֹנִי

south	darom	דָרוֹם (ז)
to the south	da'roma	דָרוֹמָה
in the south	badarom	בַּדָרוֹם
southern (adj)	dromi	דְרוֹמִי

west	ma'arav	מַעֲרָב (ז)
to the west	ma'a'rava	מַעֲרָבָה
in the west	bama'arav	בַּמַּעֲרָב
western (adj)	ma'aravi	מַעֲרָבִי

east	mizraχ	מִזְרָח (ז)
to the east	miz'raχa	מִזְרָחָה
in the east	bamizraχ	בַּמִזְרָח
eastern (adj)	mizraχi	מִזְרָחִי

77. Sea. Ocean

sea	yam	יָם (ז)
ocean	ok'yanos	אוֹקְיָאנוֹס (ז)
gulf (bay)	mifrats	מִפְרָץ (ז)
straits	meitsar	מֵיצָר (ז)

land (solid ground)	yabaʃa	יַבָּשָׁה (נ)
continent (mainland)	ya'beʃet	יַבֶּשֶׁת (נ)
island	i	אִי (ז)
peninsula	χatsi i	חֲצִי אִי (ז)
archipelago	arχipelag	אַרְכִיפֶּלָג (ז)

bay, cove	mifrats	מִפְרָץ (ז)
harbor	namal	נָמָל (ז)
lagoon	la'guna	לָגוּנָה (נ)
cape	kef	כֵּף (ז)

atoll	atol	אָטוֹל (ז)
reef	ʃunit	שׁוּנִית (נ)
coral	almog	אַלְמוֹג (ז)
coral reef	ʃunit almogim	שׁוּנִית אַלְמוֹגִים (נ)

deep (adj)	amok	עָמוֹק
depth (deep water)	'omek	עוֹמֶק (ז)
abyss	tehom	תְּהוֹם (נ)
trench (e.g., Mariana ~)	maxteʃ	מַכְתֵּשׁ (ז)
current (Ocean ~)	'zerem	זֶרֶם (ז)
to surround (bathe)	lehakif	לְהַקִּיף
shore	χof	חוֹף (ז)
coast	χof yam	חוֹף יָם (ז)
flow (flood tide)	ge'ut	גֵּאוּת (נ)
ebb (ebb tide)	'ʃefel	שֵׁפֶל (ז)
shoal	sirton	שִׂרְטוֹן (ז)
bottom (~ of the sea)	karka'it	קַרְקָעִית (נ)
wave	gal	גַּל (ז)
crest (~ of a wave)	pisgat hagal	פִּסְגַּת הַגַּל (נ)
spume (sea foam)	'ketsef	קֶצֶף (ז)
storm (sea storm)	sufa	סוּפָה (נ)
hurricane	hurikan	הוֹרִיקָן (ז)
tsunami	tsu'nami	צוּנָאמִי (ז)
calm (dead ~)	'roga	רוֹגַע (ז)
quiet, calm (adj)	ʃalev	שָׁלֵו
pole	'kotev	קוֹטֶב (ז)
polar (adj)	kotbi	קוֹטְבִּי
latitude	kav 'roχav	קַו רוֹחַב (ז)
longitude	kav 'orex	קַו אוֹרֶךְ (ז)
parallel	kav 'roχav	קַו רוֹחַב (ז)
equator	kav hamaʃve	קַו הַמַּשְׁוֶה (ז)
sky	ʃa'mayim	שָׁמַיִם (ז"ר)
horizon	'ofek	אוֹפֶק (ז)
air	avir	אֲוִויר (ז)
lighthouse	migdalor	מִגְדַּלּוֹר (ז)
to dive (vi)	litslol	לִצְלוֹל
to sink (ab. boat)	lit'bo'a	לִטְבּוֹעַ
treasures	otsarot	אוֹצָרוֹת (ז"ר)

78. Seas' and Oceans' names

Atlantic Ocean	ha'ok'yanus ha'at'lanti	הָאוֹקְיָינוֹס הָאַטְלַנְטִי (ז)
Indian Ocean	ha'ok'yanus ha'hodi	הָאוֹקְיָינוֹס הַהוֹדִי (ז)
Pacific Ocean	ha'ok'yanus haʃaket	הָאוֹקְיָינוֹס הַשָּׁקֵט (ז)
Arctic Ocean	ok'yanos ha'keraχ hatsfoni	אוֹקְיָינוֹס הַקֶּרַח הַצְּפוֹנִי (ז)
Black Sea	hayam haʃaχor	הַיָּם הַשָּׁחוֹר (ז)

Red Sea	yam suf	יַם סוּף (ז)
Yellow Sea	hayam hatsahov	הַיָם הַצָהֹוב (ז)
White Sea	hayam halavan	הַיָם הַלָבָן (ז)
Caspian Sea	hayam ha'kaspi	הַיָם הַכַּסְפִּי (ז)
Dead Sea	yam ha'melax	יַם הַמֶלַח (ז)
Mediterranean Sea	hayam hatixon	הַיָם הַתִיכֹון (ז)
Aegean Sea	hayam ha'e'ge'i	הַיָם הָאֶגֵאִי (ז)
Adriatic Sea	hayam ha'adri'yati	הַיָם הָאַדְרִיָאתִי (ז)
Arabian Sea	hayam ha'aravi	הַיָם הָעֲרָבִי (ז)
Sea of Japan	hayam haya'pani	הַיָם הַיַפָּנִי (ז)
Bering Sea	yam 'bering	יַם בֶּרִינג (ז)
South China Sea	yam sin hadromi	יַם סִין הַדְרֹומִי (ז)
Coral Sea	yam ha'almogim	יַם הָאַלְמֹוגִים (ז)
Tasman Sea	yam tasman	יַם טַסְמַן (ז)
Caribbean Sea	hayam haka'ribi	הַיָם הַקָרִיבִּי (ז)
Barents Sea	yam 'barents	יים בָּרֶנץ (ז)
Kara Sea	yam 'kara	יַם קָאֹרָה (ז)
North Sea	hayam hatsfoni	הַיָם הַצְפֹונִי (ז)
Baltic Sea	hayam ha'balti	הַיָם הַבָּלְטִי (ז)
Norwegian Sea	hayam hanor'vegi	הַיָם הַנֹורְבֵּגִי (ז)

79. Mountains

mountain	har	הַר (ז)
mountain range	'rexes harim	רֶכֶס הָרִים (ז)
mountain ridge	'rexes har	רֶכֶס הַר (ז)
summit, top	pisga	פִּסְגָה (נ)
peak	pisga	פִּסְגָה (נ)
foot (~ of the mountain)	margelot	מַרְגְלֹות (נ"ר)
slope (mountainside)	midron	מִדְרֹון (ז)
volcano	har 'ga'aʃ	הַר גַעַש (ז)
active volcano	har 'ga'aʃ pa'il	הַר גַעַש פָּעִיל (ז)
dormant volcano	har 'ga'aʃ radum	הַר גַעַש רָדוּם (ז)
eruption	hitpartsut	הִתְפָּרְצוּת (נ)
crater	lo'a	לֹועַ (ז)
magma	megama	מָגְמָה (נ)
lava	'lava	לָאבָה (נ)
molten (~ lava)	lohet	לֹוהֵט
canyon	kanyon	קַנְיֹון (ז)
gorge	gai	גַיְא (ז)

crevice	'beka	בָּקַע (ז)
abyss (chasm)	tehom	תְּהוֹם (נ)
pass, col	ma'avar harim	מַעֲבַר הָרִים (ז)
plateau	rama	רָמָה (נ)
cliff	tsuk	צוּק (ז)
hill	giv'a	גִּבעָה (נ)
glacier	karχon	קַרחוֹן (ז)
waterfall	mapal 'mayim	מַפַּל מַיִם (ז)
geyser	'geizer	גֵּייזֶר (ז)
lake	agam	אֲגַם (ז)
plain	miʃor	מִישׁוֹר (ז)
landscape	nof	נוֹף (ז)
echo	hed	הֵד (ז)
alpinist	metapes harim	מְטַפֵּס הָרִים (ז)
rock climber	metapes sla'im	מְטַפֵּס סְלָעִים (ז)
to conquer (in climbing)	liχboʃ	לִכבּוֹשׁ
climb (an easy ~)	tipus	טִיפּוּס (ז)

80. Mountains names

The Alps	harei ha''alpim	הָרֵי הָאַלפִּים (ז"ר)
Mont Blanc	mon blan	מוֹן בְּלָאן (ז)
The Pyrenees	pire'ne'im	פִּירֶנָאִים (ז"ר)
The Carpathians	kar'patim	קַרפָּטִים (ז"ר)
The Ural Mountains	harei ural	הָרֵי אוּרָל (ז"ר)
The Caucasus Mountains	harei hakavkaz	הָרֵי הַקַווקָז (ז"ר)
Mount Elbrus	elbrus	אֶלבּרוּס (ז)
The Altai Mountains	harei altai	הָרֵי אַלטַאי (ז"ר)
The Tian Shan	tyan ʃan	טִיאָן שָׁאן (ז)
The Pamir Mountains	harei pamir	הָרֵי פָּאמִיר (ז"ר)
The Himalayas	harei hehima'laya	הָרֵי הָהִימָלָאיָה (ז"ר)
Mount Everest	everest	אֶוֶורֶסט (ז)
The Andes	harei ha''andim	הָרֵי הָאַנדִים (ז"ר)
Mount Kilimanjaro	kiliman'dʒaro	קִילִימַנגַ׳רוֹ (ז)

81. Rivers

river	nahar	נָהָר (ז)
spring (natural source)	ma'ayan	מַעִיָין (ז)
riverbed (river channel)	afik	אָפִיק (ז)
basin (river valley)	agan nahar	אַגַן נָהָר (ז)

to flow into ...	lehiʃapeχ	לְהִישָׁפֵךְ
tributary	yuval	יוּבָל (ז)
bank (of river)	χof	חוֹף (ז)
current (stream)	'zerem	זֶרֶם (ז)
downstream (adv)	bemorad hanahar	בְּמוֹרַד הַנָּהָר
upstream (adv)	bema'ale hanahar	בְּמַעֲלֵה הַזֶּרֶם
inundation	hatsafa	הַצָּפָה (נ)
flooding	ʃitafon	שִׁיטָפוֹן (ז)
to overflow (vi)	la'alot al gdotav	לַעֲלוֹת עַל גְדוֹתָיו
to flood (vt)	lehatsif	לְהָצִיף
shallow (shoal)	sirton	שִׂרְטוֹן (ז)
rapids	'eʃed	אֶשֶׁד (ז)
dam	'seχer	סֶכֶר (ז)
canal	te'ala	תְּעָלָה (נ)
reservoir (artificial lake)	ma'agar 'mayim	מַאֲגַר מַיִם (ז)
sluice, lock	ta 'ʃayit	תָּא שַׁיִט (ז)
water body (pond, etc.)	ma'agar 'mayim	מַאֲגַר מַיִם (ז)
swamp (marshland)	bitsa	בִּיצָה (נ)
bog, marsh	bitsa	בִּיצָה (נ)
whirlpool	me'ar'bolet	מְעַרְבּוֹלֶת (נ)
stream (brook)	'naχal	נַחַל (ז)
drinking (ab. water)	ʃel ʃtiya	שֶׁל שְׁתִיָה
fresh (~ water)	metukim	מְתוּקִים
ice	'keraχ	קֶרַח (ז)
to freeze over	likpo	לִקְפּוֹא
(ab. river, etc.)		

82. Rivers' names

Seine	hasen	הַסֶן (ז)
Loire	lu'ar	לוֹאָר (ז)
Thames	'temza	תֶמְזָה (נ)
Rhine	hrain	הָרַיין (ז)
Danube	da'nuba	דָנוּבָּה (ז)
Volga	'volga	וֹלְגָה (ז)
Don	nahar don	נָהָר דוֹן (ז)
Lena	'lena	לֶנָה (ז)
Yellow River	hvang ho	הוַואנג הוֹ (ז)
Yangtze	yangtse	יַאנגצֶה (ז)
Mekong	mekong	מֶקוֹנג (ז)

Ganges	'ganges	גַּנגֶּס (ז)
Nile River	'nilus	נִילוּס (ז)
Congo River	'kongo	קוֹנגוֹ (ז)
Okavango River	ok'vango	אוֹקָבַנגוֹ (ז)
Zambezi River	zam'bezi	זַמבֶּזִי (ז)
Limpopo River	limpopo	לִימפּוֹפּוֹ (ז)
Mississippi River	misi'sipi	מִיסִיסִיפִּי (ז)

83. Forest

forest, wood	'ya'ar	יַעַר (ז)
forest (as adj)	ʃel 'ya'ar	שֶׁל יַעַר
thick forest	avi ha'ya'ar	עֲבִי הַיַּעַר (ז)
grove	xurʃa	חֻורשָׁה (נ)
forest clearing	ka'raxat 'ya'ar	קָרַחַת יַעַר (נ)
thicket	svax	סְבַךְ (ז)
scrubland	'siax	שִׂיחַ (ז)
footpath (troddenpath)	ʃvil	שבִיל (ז)
gully	'emek tsar	עֵמֶק צַר (ז)
tree	ets	עֵץ (ז)
leaf	ale	עָלֶה (ז)
leaves (foliage)	alva	עַלוָוה (נ)
fall of leaves	ʃa'lexet	שַׁלֶּכֶת (נ)
to fall (ab. leaves)	linʃor	לִנשׁוֹר
top (of the tree)	tsa'meret	צַמֶּרֶת (נ)
branch	anaf	עָנָף (ז)
bough	anaf ave	עָנָף עָבֶה (ז)
bud (on shrub, tree)	nitsan	נִיצָן (ז)
needle (of pine tree)	'maxat	מַחַט (נ)
pine cone	itstrubal	אִצטרוּבָּל (ז)
hollow (in a tree)	xor ba'ets	חוֹר בָּעֵץ (ז)
nest	ken	קֵן (ז)
burrow (animal hole)	mexila	מְחִילָה (נ)
trunk	'geza	גֶּזַע (ז)
root	'ʃoreʃ	שׁוֹרֶשׁ (ז)
bark	klipa	קלִיפָּה (נ)
moss	taxav	טַחַב (ז)
to uproot (remove trees or tree stumps)	la'akor	לַעֲקוֹר
to chop down	lixrot	לִכרוֹת
to deforest (vt)	levare	לְבָרֵא

tree stump	'gedem	גֶּדֶם (ז)
campfire	medura	מְדוּרָה (נ)
forest fire	srefa	שְׂרֵיפָה (נ)
to extinguish (vt)	lexabot	לְכַבּוֹת
forest ranger	ʃomer 'ya'ar	שׁוֹמֵר יַעַר (ז)
protection	ʃmira	שְׁמִירָה (נ)
to protect (~ nature)	liʃmor	לִשְׁמוֹר
poacher	tsayad lelo reʃut	צַיָּד לְלֹא רְשׁוּת (ז)
steel trap	mal'kodet	מַלְכּוֹדֶת (נ)
to gather, to pick (vt)	lelaket	לְלַקֵּט
to lose one's way	lit'ot	לִתְעוֹת

84. Natural resources

natural resources	otsarot 'teva	אוֹצָרוֹת טֶבַע (ז"ר)
minerals	mine'ralim	מִינֵרָלִים (ז"ר)
deposits	mirbats	מִרְבָּץ (ז)
field (e.g., oilfield)	mirbats	מִרְבָּץ (ז)
to mine (extract)	lixrot	לִכְרוֹת
mining (extraction)	kriya	כְּרִיָּה (נ)
ore	afra	עַפְרָה (נ)
mine (e.g., for coal)	mixre	מִכְרֶה (ז)
shaft (mine ~)	pir	פִּיר (ז)
miner	kore	כּוֹרֶה (ז)
gas (natural ~)	gaz	גָּז (ז)
gas pipeline	tsinor gaz	צִינּוֹר גָּז (ז)
oil (petroleum)	neft	נֵפְט (ז)
oil pipeline	tsinor neft	צִינּוֹר נֵפְט (ז)
oil well	be'er neft	בְּאֵר נֵפְט (נ)
derrick (tower)	migdal ki'duax	מִגְדַּל קִידּוּחַ (ז)
tanker	mexalit	מֵיכָלִית (נ)
sand	xol	חוֹל (ז)
limestone	'even gir	אֶבֶן גִּיר (נ)
gravel	xatsats	חָצָץ (ז)
peat	kavul	כָּבוּל (ז)
clay	tit	טִיט (ז)
coal	pexam	פֶּחָם (ז)
iron (ore)	barzel	בַּרְזֶל (ז)
gold	zahav	זָהָב (ז)
silver	'kesef	כֶּסֶף (ז)
nickel	'nikel	נִיקֶל (ז)
copper	ne'xoʃet	נְחוֹשֶׁת (נ)
zinc	avats	אָבָץ (ז)

manganese	mangan	מַנְגָּן (ז)
mercury	kaspit	כַּסְפִּית (נ)
lead	o'feret	עוֹפֶרֶת (נ)
mineral	mineral	מִינֶרָל (ז)
crystal	gaviʃ	גָּבִישׁ (ז)
marble	ʃayiʃ	שַׁיִשׁ (ז)
uranium	u'ranyum	אוּרַנְיוּם (ז)

85. Weather

weather	'mezeg avir	מֶזֶג אֲוִויר (ז)
weather forecast	taxazit 'mezeg ha'avir	תַּחֲזִית מֶזֶג הָאֲוִויר (נ)
temperature	tempera'tura	טֶמְפֶּרָטוּרָה (נ)
thermometer	madxom	מַדְחוֹם (ז)
barometer	ba'rometer	בָּרוֹמֶטֶר (ז)
humid (adj)	lax	לַח
humidity	laxut	לַחוּת (נ)
heat (extreme ~)	xom	חוֹם (ז)
hot (torrid)	xam	חַם
it's hot	xam	חַם
it's warm	xamim	חָמִים
warm (moderately hot)	xamim	חָמִים
it's cold	kar	קַר
cold (adj)	kar	קַר
sun	'ʃemeʃ	שֶׁמֶשׁ (נ)
to shine (vi)	lizhor	לִזְהוֹר
sunny (day)	ʃimʃi	שִׁמְשִׁי
to come up (vi)	liz'roax	לִזְרוֹחַ
to set (vi)	liʃ'ko'a	לִשְׁקוֹעַ
cloud	anan	עָנָן (ז)
cloudy (adj)	me'unan	מְעוּנָן
rain cloud	av	עָב (ז)
somber (gloomy)	sagriri	סַגְרִירִי
rain	'geʃem	גֶּשֶׁם (ז)
it's raining	yored 'geʃem	יוֹרֵד גֶּשֶׁם
rainy (~ day, weather)	gaʃum	גָּשׁוּם
to drizzle (vi)	letaftef	לְטַפְטֵף
pouring rain	matar	מָטָר (ז)
downpour	mabul	מַבּוּל (ז)
heavy (e.g., ~ rain)	xazak	חָזָק
puddle	ʃlulit	שְׁלוּלִית (נ)
to get wet (in rain)	lehitratev	לְהִתְרַטֵּב

fog (mist)	arapel	עֲרָפֶל (ז)
foggy	me'urpal	מְעוּרְפָּל
snow	'ʃeleg	שֶׁלֶג (ז)
it's snowing	yored 'ʃeleg	יוֹרֵד שֶׁלֶג

86. Severe weather. Natural disasters

thunderstorm	sufat re'amim	סוּפַת רְעָמִים (נ)
lightning (~ strike)	barak	בָּרָק (ז)
to flash (vi)	livhok	לִבְהוֹק
thunder	'ra'am	רַעַם (ז)
to thunder (vi)	lir'om	לִרְעוֹם
it's thundering	lir'om	לִרְעוֹם
hail	barad	בָּרָד (ז)
it's hailing	yored barad	יוֹרֵד בָּרָד
to flood (vt)	lehatsif	לְהָצִיף
flood, inundation	ʃitafon	שִׁיטָפוֹן (ז)
earthquake	re'idat adama	רְעִידַת אֲדָמָה (נ)
tremor, quake	re'ida	רְעִידָה (נ)
epicenter	moked	מוֹקֵד (ז)
eruption	hitpartsut	הִתְפָּרְצוּת (נ)
lava	'lava	לָאבָה (נ)
twister	hurikan	הוֹרִיקָן (ז)
tornado	tor'nado	טוֹרְנָדוֹ (ז)
typhoon	taifun	טַייפוּן (ז)
hurricane	hurikan	הוֹרִיקָן (ז)
storm	sufa	סוּפָה (נ)
tsunami	tsu'nami	צוּנָאמִי (ז)
cyclone	tsiklon	צִיקְלוֹן (ז)
bad weather	sagrir	סַגְרִיר (ז)
fire (accident)	srefa	שְׂרֵיפָה (נ)
disaster	ason	אָסוֹן (ז)
meteorite	mete'orit	מֶטֶאוֹרִיט (ז)
avalanche	ma'polet ʃlagim	מַפּוֹלֶת שְׁלָגִים (נ)
snowslide	ma'polet ʃlagim	מַפּוֹלֶת שְׁלָגִים (נ)
blizzard	sufat ʃlagim	סוּפַת שְׁלָגִים (נ)
snowstorm	sufat ʃlagim	סוּפַת שְׁלָגִים (נ)

FAUNA

87. Mammals. Predators

predator	χayat 'teref	חַיַּת טֶרֶף (נ)
tiger	'tigris	טִיגְרִיס (ז)
lion	arye	אַרְיֵה (ז)
wolf	ze'ev	זְאֵב (ז)
fox	ʃu'al	שׁוּעָל (ז)
jaguar	yagu'ar	יָגוּאָר (ז)
leopard	namer	נָמֵר (ז)
cheetah	bardelas	בַּרְדְּלָס (ז)
black panther	panter	פַּנְתֵּר (ז)
puma	'puma	פּוּמָה (נ)
snow leopard	namer 'ʃeleg	נָמֵר שֶׁלֶג (ז)
lynx	ʃunar	שׁוּנָר (ז)
coyote	ze'ev ha'aravot	זְאֵב הָעֲרָבוֹת (ז)
jackal	tan	תַּן (ז)
hyena	tsa'vo'a	צָבוֹעַ (ז)

88. Wild animals

animal	'ba'al χayim	בַּעַל חַיִּים (ז)
beast (animal)	χaya	חַיָּה (נ)
squirrel	sna'i	סְנָאִי (ז)
hedgehog	kipod	קִיפּוֹד (ז)
hare	arnav	אַרְנָב (ז)
rabbit	ʃafan	שָׁפָן (ז)
badger	girit	גִּירִית (נ)
raccoon	dvivon	דְּבִיבוֹן (ז)
hamster	oger	אוֹגֵר (ז)
marmot	mar'mita	מַרְמִיטָה (נ)
mole	χafar'peret	חֲפַרְפֶּרֶת (נ)
mouse	aχbar	עַכְבָּר (ז)
rat	χulda	חוּלְדָּה (נ)
bat	atalef	עֲטַלֵּף (ז)
ermine	hermin	הֶרְמִין (ז)
sable	tsobel	צוֹבֶּל (ז)

marten	dalak	דֶּלֶק (ז)
weasel	χamus	חָמוֹס (ז)
mink	χorfan	חוֹרְפָּן (ז)
beaver	bone	בּוֹנֶה (ז)
otter	lutra	לוּטְרָה (נ)
horse	sus	סוּס (ז)
moose	ayal hakore	אַיָּל הַקּוֹרֵא (ז)
deer	ayal	אַיָּל (ז)
camel	gamal	גָּמָל (ז)
bison	bizon	בִּיזוֹן (ז)
aurochs	bizon ei'ropi	בִּיזוֹן אֵירוֹפִּי (ז)
buffalo	te'o	תְּאוֹ (ז)
zebra	'zebra	זֶבְּרָה (נ)
antelope	anti'lopa	אַנְטִילוֹפָּה (נ)
roe deer	ayal hakarmel	אַיָּל הַכַּרְמֶל (ז)
fallow deer	yaχmur	יַחְמוּר (ז)
chamois	ya'el	יָעֵל (ז)
wild boar	χazir bar	חֲזִיר בָּר (ז)
whale	livyatan	לִוְיָתָן (ז)
seal	'kelev yam	כֶּלֶב יָם (ז)
walrus	sus yam	סוּס יָם (ז)
fur seal	dov yam	דֹּב יָם (ז)
dolphin	dolfin	דּוֹלְפִין (ז)
bear	dov	דֹּב (ז)
polar bear	dov 'kotev	דֹּב קוֹטֶב (ז)
panda	'panda	פַּנְדָּה (נ)
monkey	kof	קוֹף (ז)
chimpanzee	ʃimpanze	שִׁימְפַּנְזֶה (נ)
orangutan	orang utan	אוֹרַנְג־אוּטָן (ז)
gorilla	go'rila	גּוֹרִילָה (נ)
macaque	makak	מָקָק (ז)
gibbon	gibon	גִּיבּוֹן (ז)
elephant	pil	פִּיל (ז)
rhinoceros	karnaf	קַרְנַף (ז)
giraffe	dʒi'rafa	גִּ׳ירָפָּה (נ)
hippopotamus	hipopotam	הִיפּוֹפּוֹטָם (ז)
kangaroo	'kenguru	קֶנְגוּרוּ (ז)
koala (bear)	ko''ala	קוֹאָלָה (ז)
mongoose	nemiya	נְמִיָּה (נ)
chinchilla	tʃin'tʃila	צִ׳ינְצִ׳ילָה (נ)
skunk	bo'eʃ	בּוֹאֵשׁ (ז)
porcupine	darban	דַּרְבָּן (ז)

89. Domestic animals

cat	χatula	חֲתוּלָה (נ)
tomcat	χatul	חָתוּל (ז)
dog	'kelev	כֶּלֶב (ז)
horse	sus	סוּס (ז)
stallion (male horse)	sus harba'a	סוּס הַרבָּעָה (ז)
mare	susa	סוּסָה (נ)
cow	para	פָּרָה (נ)
bull	ʃor	שׁוֹר (ז)
ox	ʃor	שׁוֹר (ז)
sheep (ewe)	kivsa	כִּבשָׂה (נ)
ram	'ayil	אַיִל (ז)
goat	ez	עֵז (נ)
billy goat, he-goat	'tayiʃ	תַּיִשׁ (ז)
donkey	χamor	חֲמוֹר (ז)
mule	'pered	פֶּרֶד (ז)
pig, hog	χazir	חֲזִיר (ז)
piglet	χazarzir	חֲזַרזִיר (ז)
rabbit	arnav	אַרנָב (ז)
hen (chicken)	tarne'golet	תַרנְגוֹלֶת (נ)
rooster	tarnegol	תַרנְגוֹל (ז)
duck	barvaz	בַּרוָז (ז)
drake	barvaz	בַּרוָז (ז)
goose	avaz	אַוָז (ז)
tom turkey, gobbler	tarnegol 'hodu	תַרנְגוֹל הוֹדוּ (ז)
turkey (hen)	tarne'golet 'hodu	תַרנְגוֹלֶת הוֹדוּ (נ)
domestic animals	χayot 'bayit	חַיוֹת בַּיִת (נ"ר)
tame (e.g., ~ hamster)	mevuyat	מְבוּיָת
to tame (vt)	levayet	לְבַיֵת
to breed (vt)	lehar'bi'a	לְהַרבִּיעַ
farm	χava	חַוָה (נ)
poultry	ofot 'bayit	עוֹפוֹת בַּיִת (נ"ר)
cattle	bakar	בָּקָר (ז)
herd (cattle)	'eder	עֵדֶר (ז)
stable	urva	אוּרוָה (נ)
pigpen	dir χazirim	דִיר חֲזִירִים (ז)
cowshed	'refet	רֶפֶת (נ)
rabbit hutch	arnaviya	אַרנָבִייָה (נ)
hen house	lul	לוּל (ז)

90. Birds

bird	tsipor	צִיפּוֹר (נ)
pigeon	yona	יוֹנָה (נ)
sparrow	dror	דְּרוֹר (ז)
tit (great tit)	yargazi	יַרְגָּזִי (ז)
magpie	orev neχalim	עוֹרֵב נְחָלִים (ז)
raven	orev ʃaχor	עוֹרֵב שָׁחוֹר (ז)
crow	orev afor	עוֹרֵב אָפוֹר (ז)
jackdaw	ka'ak	קָאָק (ז)
rook	orev hamizra	עוֹרֵב הַמִּזְרָע (ז)
duck	barvaz	בַּרְוָז (ז)
goose	avaz	אַוָּז (ז)
pheasant	pasyon	פַסיוֹן (ז)
eagle	'ayit	עַיְט (ז)
hawk	nets	נֵץ (ז)
falcon	baz	בַּז (ז)
vulture	ozniya	עוֹזנִיָּה (נ)
condor (Andean ~)	kondor	קוֹנדוֹר (ז)
swan	barbur	בַּרְבּוּר (ז)
crane	agur	עָגוּר (ז)
stork	χasida	חֲסִידָה (נ)
parrot	'tuki	תּוּכִּי (ז)
hummingbird	ko'libri	קוֹלִיבְּרִי (ז)
peacock	tavas	טַוָּס (ז)
ostrich	bat ya'ana	בַּת יַעֲנָה (נ)
heron	anafa	אֲנָפָה (נ)
flamingo	fla'mingo	פְלָמִינגוֹ (ז)
pelican	saknai	שַׂקְנַאי (ז)
nightingale	zamir	זָמִיר (ז)
swallow	snunit	סנוּנִית (נ)
thrush	kiχli	קִיכלִי (ז)
song thrush	kiχli mezamer	קִיכלִי מְזַמֵּר (ז)
blackbird	kiχli ʃaχor	קִיכלִי שָׁחוֹר (ז)
swift	sis	סִיס (ז)
lark	efroni	עָפְרוֹנִי (ז)
quail	slav	שְׂלָיו (ז)
woodpecker	'neker	נָקָר (ז)
cuckoo	kukiya	קוּקִיָּה (נ)
owl	yanʃuf	יַנשׁוּף (ז)
eagle owl	'oaχ	אוֹחַ (ז)

wood grouse	seχvi 'ya'ar	שְׂכְוִי יַעַר (ז)
black grouse	seχvi	שְׂכְוִי (ז)
partridge	χogla	חוֹגְלָה (נ)
starling	zarzir	זַרְזִיר (ז)
canary	ka'narit	קָנָרִית (נ)
hazel grouse	seχvi haya'arot	שְׂכְוִי הַיְּעָרוֹת (ז)
chaffinch	paroʃ	פָּרוֹשׁ (ז)
bullfinch	admonit	אַדְמוֹנִית (נ)
seagull	'ʃaχaf	שַׁחַף (ז)
albatross	albatros	אַלְבַּטְרוֹס (ז)
penguin	pingvin	פִּינְגְּוִין (ז)

91. Fish. Marine animals

bream	avroma	אַבְרוֹמָה (נ)
carp	karpiyon	קַרְפִּיוֹן (ז)
perch	'okunus	אוֹקוּנוּס (ז)
catfish	sfamnun	שְׂפַמְנוּן (ז)
pike	ze'ev 'mayim	זְאֵב מַיִם (ז)
salmon	'salmon	סַלְמוֹן (ז)
sturgeon	χidkan	חִדְקָן (ז)
herring	ma'liaχ	מָלִיחַ (ז)
Atlantic salmon	iltit	אִילְתִּית (נ)
mackerel	makarel	מָקָרֶל (ז)
flatfish	dag moʃe ra'benu	דַּג מֹשֶׁה רַבֵּנוּ (ז)
zander, pike perch	amnun	אַמְנוּן (ז)
cod	ʃibut	שִׁיבּוּט (ז)
tuna	'tuna	טוּנָה (נ)
trout	forel	פּוֹרֶל (ז)
eel	tslofaχ	צְלוֹפָח (ז)
electric ray	trisanit	תְּרִיסָנִית (נ)
moray eel	mo'rena	מוֹרֶנָה (נ)
piranha	pi'ranya	פִּירַנְיָה (נ)
shark	kariʃ	כָּרִישׁ (ז)
dolphin	dolfin	דּוֹלְפִּין (ז)
whale	livyatan	לִוְיָתָן (ז)
crab	sartan	סַרְטָן (ז)
jellyfish	me'duza	קָדוּזָה (נ)
octopus	tamnun	תַּמְנוּן (ז)
starfish	koχav yam	כּוֹכַב יָם (ז)
sea urchin	kipod yam	קִיפּוֹד יָם (ז)

seahorse	suson yam	סוּסוֹן יָם (ז)
oyster	tsidpa	צִדְפָּה (נ)
shrimp	χasilon	חָסִילוֹן (ז)
lobster	'lobster	לוֹבּסטֶר (ז)
spiny lobster	'lobster kotsani	לוֹבּסטֶר קוֹצָנִי (ז)

92. Amphibians. Reptiles

snake	naχaʃ	נָחָשׁ (ז)
venomous (snake)	arsi	אַרסִי
viper	'tsefa	צֶפַע (ז)
cobra	'peten	פֶּתֶן (ז)
python	piton	פִּיתוֹן (ז)
boa	χanak	חֶנֶק (ז)
grass snake	naχaʃ 'mayim	נָחָשׁ מַיִם (ז)
rattle snake	ʃfifon	שׁפִיפוֹן (ז)
anaconda	ana'konda	אָנָקוֹנדָה (נ)
lizard	leta'a	לטָאָה (נ)
iguana	igu''ana	אִיגוּאָנָה (נ)
monitor lizard	'koaχ	כּוֹחַ (ז)
salamander	sala'mandra	סָלָמַנדרָה (נ)
chameleon	zikit	זִיקִית (נ)
scorpion	akrav	עַקרָב (ז)
turtle	tsav	צָב (ז)
frog	tsfar'de'a	צפַרדֵעַ (נ)
toad	karpada	קַרפָּדָה (נ)
crocodile	tanin	תַּנִין (ז)

93. Insects

insect, bug	χarak	חָרָק (ז)
butterfly	parpar	פַּרפַּר (ז)
ant	nemala	נמָלָה (נ)
fly	zvuv	זבוּב (ז)
mosquito	yatuʃ	יַתוּשׁ (ז)
beetle	χipuʃit	חִיפּוּשִׁית (נ)
wasp	tsir'a	צִרעָה (נ)
bee	dvora	דבוֹרָה (נ)
bumblebee	dabur	דַבּוּר (ז)
gadfly (botfly)	zvuv hasus	זבוּב הַסוּס (ז)
spider	akaviʃ	עַכָּבִישׁ (ז)
spiderweb	kurei akaviʃ	קוּרֵי עַכָּבִישׁ (ז"ר)

dragonfly	ʃapirit	שְׁפִּירִית (נ)
grasshopper	χagav	חָגָב (ז)
moth (night butterfly)	aʃ	עָשׁ (ז)
cockroach	makak	מַקָּק (ז)
tick	kartsiya	קַרְצִיָּה (נ)
flea	par'oʃ	פַּרְעוֹשׁ (ז)
midge	yavχuʃ	יַבְחוּשׁ (ז)
locust	arbe	אַרְבֶּה (ז)
snail	χilazon	חִלָּזוֹן (ז)
cricket	tsartsar	צְרָצַר (ז)
lightning bug	gaχlilit	גַּחְלִילִית (נ)
ladybug	parat moʃe ra'benu	פָּרַת מֹשֶׁה רַבֵּנוּ (נ)
cockchafer	χipuʃit aviv	חִיפוּשִׁית אָבִיב (נ)
leech	aluka	עֲלוּקָה (נ)
caterpillar	zaχal	זַחַל (ז)
earthworm	to'la'at	תּוֹלַעַת (נ)
larva	'deren	דֶּרֶן (ז)

FLORA

94. Trees

tree	ets	עֵץ (ז)
deciduous (adj)	naʃir	נָשִׁיר
coniferous (adj)	maxtani	מַחְטָנִי
evergreen (adj)	yarok ad	יָרֹק עַד
apple tree	ta'puax	תַּפּוּחַ (ז)
pear tree	agas	אַגָּס (ז)
sweet cherry tree	gudgedan	גּוּדְגְּדָן (ז)
sour cherry tree	duvdevan	דּוּבְדְּבָן (ז)
plum tree	ʃezif	שְׁזִיף (ז)
birch	ʃadar	שְׁדָר (ז)
oak	alon	אַלּוֹן (ז)
linden tree	'tilya	טִילְיָה (נ)
aspen	aspa	אַסְפָּה (נ)
maple	'eder	אֶדֶר (ז)
spruce	a'ʃuax	אַשּׁוּחַ (ז)
pine	'oren	אוֹרֶן (ז)
larch	arzit	אַרְזִית (נ)
fir tree	a'ʃuax	אַשּׁוּחַ (ז)
cedar	'erez	אֶרֶז (ז)
poplar	tsaftsefa	צַפְצָפָה (נ)
rowan	ben xuzrar	בֶּן־חוּזְרָר (ז)
willow	arava	עֲרָבָה (נ)
alder	alnus	אַלְנוּס (ז)
beech	aʃur	אַשּׁוּר (ז)
elm	bu'kitsa	בּוּקִיצָה (נ)
ash (tree)	mela	מֵילָה (נ)
chestnut	armon	עַרְמוֹן (ז)
magnolia	mag'nolya	מַגְנוֹלְיָה (נ)
palm tree	'dekel	דֶּקֶל (ז)
cypress	broʃ	בְּרוֹשׁ (ז)
mangrove	mangrov	מַנְגְּרוֹב (ז)
baobab	ba'obab	בָּאוֹבָּב (ז)
eucalyptus	eika'liptus	אֵיקָלִיפְּטוּס (ז)
sequoia	sek'voya	סֶקְווֹיָה (נ)

95. Shrubs

bush	'siax	שִׂיחַ (ז)
shrub	'siax	שִׂיחַ (ז)
grapevine	'gefen	גֶּפֶן (ז)
vineyard	'kerem	כֶּרֶם (ז)
raspberry bush	'petel	פֶּטֶל (ז)
blackcurrant bush	'siax dumdemaniyot ʃxorot	שִׂיחַ דּוּמְדְּמָנִיּוֹת שְׁחוֹרוֹת (ז)
redcurrant bush	'siax dumdemaniyot adumot	שִׂיחַ דּוּמְדְּמָנִיּוֹת אֲדוּמּוֹת (ז)
gooseberry bush	xazarzar	חֲזַרְזַר (ז)
acacia	ʃita	שִׁיטָה (נ)
barberry	berberis	בֶּרְבֶּרִיס (ז)
jasmine	yasmin	יַסְמִין (ז)
juniper	ar'ar	עַרְעָר (ז)
rosebush	'siax vradim	שִׂיחַ וְרָדִים (ז)
dog rose	'vered bar	וֶרֶד בָּר (ז)

96. Fruits. Berries

fruit	pri	פְּרִי (ז)
fruits	perot	פֵּירוֹת (ז"ר)
apple	ta'puax	תַּפּוּחַ (ז)
pear	agas	אַגָּס (ז)
plum	ʃezif	שְׁזִיף (ז)
strawberry (garden ~)	tut sade	תּוּת שָׂדֶה (ז)
sour cherry	duvdevan	דּוּבְדְּבָן (ז)
sweet cherry	gudgedan	גּוּדְגְּדָן (ז)
grape	anavim	עֲנָבִים (ז"ר)
raspberry	'petel	פֶּטֶל (ז)
blackcurrant	dumdemanit ʃxora	דּוּמְדְּמָנִית שְׁחוֹרָה (נ)
redcurrant	dumdemanit aduma	דּוּמְדְּמָנִית אֲדוּמָּה (נ)
gooseberry	xazarzar	חֲזַרְזַר (ז)
cranberry	xamutsit	חֲמוּצִית (נ)
orange	tapuz	תַּפּוּז (ז)
mandarin	klemen'tina	קְלֶמֶנְטִינָה (נ)
pineapple	'ananas	אֲנָנָס (ז)
banana	ba'nana	בַּנָנָה (נ)
date	tamar	תָּמָר (ז)
lemon	limon	לִימוֹן (ז)
apricot	'miʃmeʃ	מִשְׁמֵשׁ (ז)

peach	afarsek	אֲפַרְסֵק (ז)
kiwi	'kivi	קִיוִוי (ז)
grapefruit	eʃkolit	אֶשְׁכּוֹלִית (נ)
berry	garger	גַּרְגֵּר (ז)
berries	gargerim	גַּרְגְּרִים (ז"ר)
cowberry	uχmanit aduma	אוּכְמָנִית אֲדוּמָה (נ)
wild strawberry	tut 'ya'ar	תּוּת יַעַר (ז)
bilberry	uχmanit	אוּכְמָנִית (נ)

97. Flowers. Plants

flower	'peraχ	פֶּרַח (ז)
bouquet (of flowers)	zer	זֵר (ז)
rose (flower)	'vered	וֶרֶד (ז)
tulip	tsiv'oni	צִבְעוֹנִי (ז)
carnation	tsi'poren	צִיפּוֹרֶן (ז)
gladiolus	glad'yola	גְּלָדִיוֹלָה (נ)
cornflower	dganit	דְּגָנִית (נ)
harebell	pa'amonit	פַּעֲמוֹנִית (נ)
dandelion	ʃinan	שִׁינָן (ז)
camomile	kamomil	קָמוֹמִיל (ז)
aloe	alvai	אַלְוַוי (ז)
cactus	'kaktus	קַקְטוּס (ז)
rubber plant, ficus	'fikus	פִיקוּס (ז)
lily	ʃoʃana	שׁוֹשַׁנָּה (נ)
geranium	ge'ranyum	גֵּרַנְיוּם (ז)
hyacinth	yakinton	יָקִינְטוֹן (ז)
mimosa	mi'moza	מִימוֹזָה (נ)
narcissus	narkis	נַרְקִיס (ז)
nasturtium	'kova hanazir	כּוֹבַע הַנָּזִיר (ז)
orchid	saχlav	סַחְלָב (ז)
peony	admonit	אַדְמוֹנִית (נ)
violet	sigalit	סִיגָלִית (נ)
pansy	amnon vetamar	אַמְנוֹן וְתָמָר (ז)
forget-me-not	ziχ'rini	זִכְרִינִי (ז)
daisy	marganit	מַרְגָּנִית (נ)
poppy	'pereg	פֶּרֶג (ז)
hemp	ka'nabis	קָנַאבִּיס (ז)
mint	'menta	מֶנְתָּה (נ)
lily of the valley	zivanit	זִיוָנִית (נ)
snowdrop	ga'lantus	גָּלַנְטוּס (ז)

nettle	sirpad	סִרְפָּד (ז)
sorrel	χum'a	חוּמְעָה (נ)
water lily	nufar	נוּפָר (ז)
fern	ʃaraχ	שָׁרָךְ (ז)
lichen	χazazit	חֲזָזִית (נ)

greenhouse (tropical ~)	χamama	חֲמָמָה (נ)
lawn	midʃa'a	מִדְשָׁאָה (נ)
flowerbed	arugat praχim	עֲרוּגַת פְּרָחִים (נ)

plant	'tsemaχ	צֶמַח (ז)
grass	'deʃe	דֶשֶׁא (ז)
blade of grass	giv'ol 'esev	גִבְעוֹל עֵשֶׂב (ז)

leaf	ale	עָלֶה (ז)
petal	ale ko'teret	עָלֶה כּוֹתֶרֶת (ז)
stem	giv'ol	גִבְעוֹל (ז)
tuber	'pka'at	פְּקַעַת (נ)

| young plant (shoot) | 'nevet | נֶבֶט (ז) |
| thorn | kots | קוֹץ (ז) |

to blossom (vi)	lif'roaχ	לִפְרוֹחַ
to fade, to wither	linbol	לִנְבּוֹל
smell (odor)	'reaχ	רֵיחַ (ז)
to cut (flowers)	ligzom	לִגְזוֹם
to pick (a flower)	liktof	לִקְטוֹף

98. Cereals, grains

grain	tvu'a	תְּבוּאָה (נ)
cereal crops	dganim	דְגָנִים (ז"ר)
ear (of barley, etc.)	ʃi'bolet	שִׁיבּוֹלֶת (נ)

wheat	χita	חִיטָה (נ)
rye	ʃifon	שִׁיפוֹן (ז)
oats	ʃi'bolet ʃu'al	שִׁיבּוֹלֶת שׁוּעָל (נ)

| millet | 'doχan | דוֹחַן (ז) |
| barley | se'ora | שְׂעוֹרָה (נ) |

corn	'tiras	תִּירָס (ז)
rice	'orez	אוֹרֶז (ז)
buckwheat	ku'semet	כּוּסֶמֶת (נ)

pea plant	afuna	אֲפוּנָה (נ)
kidney bean	ʃu'it	שְׁעוּעִית (נ)
soy	'soya	סוֹיָה (נ)
lentil	adaʃim	עֲדָשִׁים (ז"ר)
beans (pulse crops)	pol	פּוֹל (ז)

COUNTRIES OF THE WORLD

99. Countries. Part 1

Afghanistan	afganistan	אַפגָנִיסטָן (נ)
Albania	al'banya	אַלבַּנִיָה (נ)
Argentina	argen'tina	אַרגֶנטִינָה (נ)
Armenia	ar'menya	אַרמֶנִיָה (נ)
Australia	ost'ralya	אוֹסטרַלִיָה (נ)
Austria	'ostriya	אוֹסטרִיָה (נ)
Azerbaijan	azerbaidʒan	אָזֶרבַּייגָ'ן (נ)
The Bahamas	iyey ba'hama	אִיֵי בָּהָאמָה (ז"ר)
Bangladesh	bangladeʃ	בַּנגלָדֶש (נ)
Belarus	'belarus	בֶּלָרוּס (נ)
Belgium	'belgya	בֶּלגִיָה (נ)
Bolivia	bo'livya	בּוֹלִיבִיָה (נ)
Bosnia and Herzegovina	'bosniya	בּוֹסנִיָה (נ)
Brazil	brazil	בּרָזִיל (נ)
Bulgaria	bul'garya	בּוּלגַרִיָה (נ)
Cambodia	kam'bodya	קַמבּוֹדִיָה (נ)
Canada	'kanada	קָנָדָה (נ)
Chile	'tʃile	צִ'ילֶה (נ)
China	sin	סִין (נ)
Colombia	ko'lombya	קוֹלוֹמבִּיָה (נ)
Croatia	kro"atya	קרוֹאַטִיָה (נ)
Cuba	'kuba	קוּבָּה (נ)
Cyprus	kafrisin	קַפרִיסִין (נ)
Czech Republic	'tʃeχya	צֶ'כִיָה (נ)
Denmark	'denemark	דֶנֶמַרק (נ)
Dominican Republic	hare'publika hadomeni'kanit	הָרֶפּוּבּלִיקָה הַדוֹמִינִיקָנִית (נ)
Ecuador	ekvador	אֶקוָודוֹר (נ)
Egypt	mits'rayim	מִצרַיִם (נ)
England	'angliya	אַנגלִיָה (נ)
Estonia	es'tonya	אֶסטוֹנִיָה (נ)
Finland	'finland	פִינלַנד (נ)
France	tsarfat	צָרפַת (נ)
French Polynesia	poli'nezya hatsarfatit	פּוֹלִינֶזיָה הַצָרפָתִית (נ)
Georgia	'gruzya	גרוּזִיָה (נ)
Germany	ger'manya	גֶרמַנִיָה (נ)
Ghana	'gana	גָאנָה (נ)
Great Britain	bri'tanya hagdola	בּרִיטַנִיָה הַגדוֹלָה (נ)

Greece	yavan	יָוָן (נ)
Haiti	ha''iti	הָאִיטִי (נ)
Hungary	hun'garya	הוֹנגַריָה (נ)

100. Countries. Part 2

Iceland	'island	אִיסלַנד (נ)
India	'hodu	הוֹדוּ (נ)
Indonesia	indo'nezya	אִינדוֹנֶזיָה (נ)
Iran	iran	אִירָן (נ)
Iraq	irak	עִירָאק (נ)
Ireland	'irland	אִירלַנד (נ)
Israel	yisra'el	יִשׂרָאֵל (נ)
Italy	i'talya	אִיטַליָה (נ)

Jamaica	dʒa'maika	גָ'מַייקה (נ)
Japan	yapan	יַפָּן (נ)
Jordan	yarden	יַרדֵן (נ)
Kazakhstan	kazaχstan	קָזַחסטָן (נ)
Kenya	'kenya	קֶניָה (נ)
Kirghizia	kirgizstan	קִירגִיזסטָן (נ)
Kuwait	kuveit	כּוּוֵית (נ)

Laos	la'os	לָאוֹס (נ)
Latvia	'latviya	לַטבִיָה (נ)
Lebanon	levanon	לְבָנוֹן (נ)
Libya	luv	לוב (נ)
Liechtenstein	liχtenʃtain	לִיכטֶנשטַיין (נ)
Lithuania	'lita	לִיטָא (נ)
Luxembourg	luksemburg	לוקסֶמבּוּרג (נ)

Macedonia (Republic of ~)	make'donya	מָקֶדוֹניָה (נ)
Madagascar	madagaskar	מָדָגַסקָר (ז)
Malaysia	ma'lezya	מָלֶזיָה (נ)
Malta	'malta	מַלטָה (נ)
Mexico	'meksiko	מֶקסִיקוֹ (נ)
Moldova, Moldavia	mol'davya	מוֹלדַביָה (נ)

Monaco	mo'nako	מוֹנָקוֹ (נ)
Mongolia	mon'golya	מוֹנגוֹליָה (נ)
Montenegro	monte'negro	מוֹנטֶנֶגרוֹ (נ)
Morocco	ma'roko	מָרוֹקוֹ (נ)
Myanmar	miyanmar	מיַאנמָר (נ)

Namibia	na'mibya	נָמִיבּיָה (נ)
Nepal	nepal	נֶפָּאל (נ)
Netherlands	'holand	הוֹלַנד (נ)
New Zealand	nyu 'ziland	ניו זִילַנד (נ)
North Korea	ko'rei'a hatsfonit	קוֹרִיאָה הַצפוֹנִית (נ)
Norway	nor'vegya	נוֹרבֶגיָה (נ)

101. Countries. Part 3

Pakistan	pakistan	פָּקִיסטָן (נ)
Palestine	falastin	פָלַסטִין (נ)
Panama	pa'nama	פָּנָמָה (נ)
Paraguay	paragvai	פָּרָגווַאי (נ)
Peru	peru	פֶּרוּ (נ)
Poland	polin	פּוֹלִין (נ)
Portugal	portugal	פּוֹרטוּגָל (נ)
Romania	ro'manya	רוֹמַניָה (נ)
Russia	'rusya	רוּסיָה (נ)
Saudi Arabia	arav hasa'udit	עֲרָב הַסָעוּדִית (נ)
Scotland	'skotland	סקוֹטלַנד (נ)
Senegal	senegal	סֶנֶגָל (נ)
Serbia	'serbya	סֶרבִּיָה (נ)
Slovakia	slo'vakya	סלוֹבָקיָה (נ)
Slovenia	slo'venya	סלוֹבֶניָה (נ)
South Africa	drom 'afrika	דרוֹם אַפרִיקָה (נ)
South Korea	ko'rei'a hadromit	קוֹרֵיאָה הַדרוֹמִית (נ)
Spain	sfarad	סְפָרַד (נ)
Suriname	surinam	סוּרִינָאם (נ)
Sweden	'ʃvedya	שבֶדיָה (נ)
Switzerland	'ʃvaits	שוַויץ (נ)
Syria	'surya	סוּריָה (נ)
Taiwan	taivan	טַייווָן (נ)
Tajikistan	tadʒikistan	טָג'יקִיסטָן (נ)
Tanzania	tan'zanya	טַנזַניָה (נ)
Tasmania	tas'manya	טַסמַניָה (נ)
Thailand	'tailand	תַאִילַנד (נ)
Tunisia	tu'nisya	טוּנִיסיָה (נ)
Turkey	'turkiya	טוּרקיָה (נ)
Turkmenistan	turkmenistan	טוּרקמֶנִיסטָן (נ)
Ukraine	uk'rayna	אוּקרַאִינָה (נ)
United Arab Emirates	iχud ha'emi'royot	אִיחוּד הָאֵמִירוּיוֹת
	ha'araviyot	הָעֲרָביוֹת (ז)
United States of America	artsot habrit	אַרצוֹת הַבּרִית (נ"ר)
Uruguay	urugvai	אוּרוּגווַאי (נ)
Uzbekistan	uzbekistan	אוּזבָּקִיסטָן (נ)
Vatican	vatikan	וָתִיקָן (ז)
Venezuela	venetsu"ela	וֶנֶצוּאֶלָה (נ)
Vietnam	vyetnam	וִייֶטנָאם (נ)
Zanzibar	zanzibar	זַנזִיבָּר (נ)

www.ingramcontent.com/pod-product-compliance
Lightning Source LLC
Chambersburg PA
CBHW070815050426
42452CB00011B/2060